The Mongo's Guide to

Skateboarding

Published by
CheapSkate Press
an imprint of
17th Street Productions
an Alloy Online, Inc. company
151 West 26th Street
11th Floor
New York, NY 10011

CheapSkate Press books published in
association with LPC Group

Copyright © 2001 by 17th Street Productions
and Ben Bermudez
Cover copyright © 2001 17th Street Productions
Cover photography by Frank Galland
Book design by Jay Hacioglu
Illustrations by DCWallin

CheapSkate Press is a trademark of 17th Street
Productions, an Alloy Online, Inc. company. All
rights reserved.

ISBN: 1-931497-42-7

Manufactured in Hong Kong

First CheapSkate Press Books printing
September 2001

10 9 8 7 6 5 4 3 2 1

To Sailine Knutz

Introduction

Skateboarding = Life

Yo. Welcome to Skate: The Mongo's Guide to Skateboarding. If you bought this book, it's probably because you want to learn how to skateboard. Congratulations. If you bought this book expecting to learn how to in-line skate or ride one of those trendy little scooters your mommy rides, then you should ask for a refund. My advice to you is to keep this book and learn how to skateboard instead. In the following pages you'll learn how to talk like a skater, how to eat like a skater, how to prevent "swellbow" (see page 21)—and most importantly, how to do really cool tricks.

I started skating when I was seven years old. My grandparents bought my first board for me. I used to push down an alley for hours, trying to learn ollies (see page 48). At first I thought of the skateboard as a toy, but it quickly became my whole life. I would spend all of my free time skateboarding, watching skateboard videos, reading skateboard magazines, and drawing skateboard logos and pictures. Sure, I was a little obsessed. But the way I figured it, better that I was obsessed with skateboarding than beating people up or playing with stuffed animals.

When you skate, you see things differently. Most people are pretty small-minded about their environment. When they look at stairs, curbs, ledges, handrails, and gaps, they just see some boring urban scenery. But when skateboarders look at these things, they see limitless possibilities—like how these obstacles can be used for tricks, how they can be tagged with graffiti. . . It's just so amazing. I still trip out on it every day. I mean, skateboarding can open so many doors and possibilities: new friends, new music—even job opportunities. No joke. I work for a skateboard company. If I didn't skate, I'd be on welfare right now.

The sad thing is a lot of people frown on skateboarding. Parents, especially. A lot of them think of it as just a hobby. They may even ask you to give it up. But why? That's not fair. You wouldn't ask them to give up their bridge game, would you? If they get down on you, just remember what you can get out of skateboarding. Style. Flow. Respect. Remember how it can turn you into the baddest mutha on the block.

When people ask me if I'm ever going to give up skateboarding, I tell them that I'll give it up when I'm physically unable to do it anymore. But that'll be in the future, and hopefully by that time I'll have an artificial body. —B. B.

contents

The Mongo

Meet The Mongo. He is your guide, and he represents many things. In one way, he represents all that is straight silly in skateboarding. His name originated from the dumbest way to push (see page 42-45). Pushing mongo is the first mistake most beginners make. Guaranteed, if you're a beginner, and you're all set to ride your first board, you will push mongo. The Mongo also represents the simple folk. He doesn't have much of an education, so he explains skateboarding in a way that almost every dummy can understand. Finally, The Mongo represents you: the kid whose mommy wants you to have Rollerblades instead of a skateboard. Over the course of this book, however, The Mongo will acquire wisdom and knowledge, and he will never, ever in-line skate or mongo again. And you will follow in his path.

With that said, always remember Rule #1 of skateboarding: Enjoy it!

USKA
SHORTY'S
SKATEBOARDS

The Mongo's Guide to buying a Skateboard

Obviously, you can't skate if you don't have a board. You have two options: you can buy a board that has already been assembled for you, or you can build one yourself. I highly recommend building one yourself because then you know exactly what you'll be riding. It'll represent you. Rule #2 of skateboarding: Individuality is key. Besides, you can't ride some totally wack, mass-produced, supermarket board—not unless you want to get laughed out of every skate park. In this chapter you will learn about the different parts of the skateboard: how much the good stuff costs, what each part does, and how to choose among types. Then you can go bug your mom for the cash to buy it all.

The Deck

Deck: The part of the board you stand on. Generally made up of seven layers of maple wood that are glued and pressed together.

Concave: A curved deck, as opposed to a flat one. The shape doesn't enhance performance; some skateboarders just prefer the look.

Wheelbase: The distance on your deck between the front four truckmounting holes and the back four truckmounting holes (see page 14 for definition of truck).

Choosing the right deck can be hard, especially if you don't know what you like. There are different widths, lengths, wheelbases, and graphics. (Graphics don't really matter, but if you can find a deck with a sick design, then obviously you're hyped. Check out **The Incomplete Graphics Guide** below.) If you don't know what shape you like, you should base your decision on your own dimensions: your foot size, height, weight, ugliness . . . (nah, you're all just a little rough around the edges). The brand you choose isn't as important as finding the right shape, but take into consideration that most of the established companies have been making skateboards for years—and they use only the best woods and glues to give you a better product. I use a **Shorty's Muska 7.5-inch deck**, but that's just my preference. It's good for both street and ramp skating (see below) and costs around $55. Shorty's makes a killer board.

The Incomplete Graphics Guide
(Alphabetical by Deck-Manufacturing Company)

IMPORTANT NOTE: This guide is incomplete for a few reasons. First of all, we couldn't possibly list all the deck-manufacturing companies in the world. Chances are that in your hometown, some underground company—or maybe even just a random skate freak—makes killer decks with sick designs. Listed here are just a few of the most popular companies. Also, while we tried to pick a graphic that generally represents each company's style, there are exceptions to every rule. For a complete picture, go to a skate shop or subscribe to a skateboard catalog. (CCS puts out a good one.)

Baker: Punk rock at its worst.

Birdhouse: Cartoon graphics with funny themes.

Black Label: Classic logos and designs, always with the Lucero theme.

Blind: Don't fear the reaper.

a Skateboard

Darkstar: All their decks pretty much have the Darkstar knights on them.
Element: Generally, these decks kick the hieroglyphic or pattern vibe.
Flip: Subliminal messages.
Girl: Sometimes they have the women's room sign on 'em; sometimes they don't.
Hook-Ups: Beautiful japanimation girls.
Powell: The angry, angelic kid.
Shorty's: Crazy graphics; sometimes shops won't even carry their products. But they also have some more mellow stuff.
Think: San Francisco—based graphics with their classic tag logo.
Toy Machine: American flags, demonic monsters … pretty much all over the place.
World Industries: Cartoon evil vs. cartoon good. Who will win?
Zero: Death! Blood! Generally a metal theme. A lot of black.

Think

World Industries

Darkstar

Blind

Listed here are suggested deck specs for different styles and terrains.

Street Decks

Street skating consists of skateboarding curbs, ledges, gaps, stairs, and rails. It also includes flip tricks. The majority of street skaters prefer deck widths ranging from 7.5 to 8 inches, with an average length of 31 to 32 inches. Wheelbases, like deck shapes, are a matter of personal preference; you won't even notice the difference between types until you've ridden many different boards. The dimensions above are preferred by most street skateboarders for one simple reason: they've been proven to be the most functional for this type of skateboarding. (By the way: If you're a really small kid, you might just want to ride a minideck.)

Half-Pipe, Miniramp, Vert-Ramp, and Pool Decks

Half Pipe: A U-shaped ramp, specifically designed for skateboarding—you roll down one side and roll up the other.
Miniramp: Designed as a half pipe but smaller than average and given a flatter bottom. Not as fast.
Vert Ramp: A twelve-foot-tall half pipe with a foot or more of vertical wall on each side.
Pool: A nice place to swim. If there's no water, a good place to skate.

When skating ramps, you might want to have a wider deck than what you would use in the streets. The average miniramp, pool, or vert deck width ranges from 7.75 to 8.5 inches, with an average length of 31 to 32 inches. If you're a smaller guy or girl, you are not going to want an 8.5-inch deck. You're probably better off with something ranging from 7.75 to 8 inches. The wider-size deck is preferred here because when skating these terrains, you're not doing the technical skateboarding you would be doing on a street deck.

All-Terrain Decks

The truth is, if you're way comfortable on the board you have, you can ride almost anything. But for the average person who skates any terrain, the deck widths are generally 7.75 to 8 inches. It's just a matter of what makes you feel most comfortable.

Cruising

It never hurts to have a cruiser board. These are boards specifically designed so that cracks, rocks, and fat ladies are not issues. Sometimes you just want to push down to the store or get somewhere without having to worry about cracks. When choosing a cruiser deck, the wider the better. You probably won't be doing any tricks on this board, so you want as much room as possible. You can even take your friends for a ride on your board if it's wide enough.

Wheels

Urethane: The plastic used to make wheels.
Durometer: A measurement of hardness. The larger the durometer number, the harder the wheel. The measurement is always followed by the letter a. (Why, I'm not sure.)

Again, choosing a wheel is just a matter of finding what you like. Sometimes heavier and harder wheels are better, sometimes not. Don't fall for gimmicks. If you hear people talking about "dual durometers"—a set of wheels with different levels of hardness—they're trying to hustle you. All wheels should have the same durometer. Check out a skate shop and see what people buy. I prefer **Ghetto Child 52-millimeter (mm) wheels** because they're hard and small, good for tricks—but that's just me. They cost about $32 a set.

Street Wheels

When skating street, most people prefer to have a lighter setup. The average street wheel ranges from 50 to 55 mm with a durometer range of 95a to 101a. The durometer and size depend on the conditions of your streets. If you live in an area where the streets are filled with potholes, you might want to ride a wheel that's 54 to 55 mm with a 95a to 97a durometer. That way you have less of a chance wiping out when you hit cracks or rocks. If you live in a place where conditions are good, a 99a to 101a durometer is preferred. A hard wheel is solid and rolls pretty fast on good terrain. One thing to keep in mind: The bigger the wheels, the harder the flip and ledge tricks. (You'll see what I mean later on in the book.) When you add more weight to your skateboard, you have that much more to get off the ground. So stay away from those doughnuts, all right?

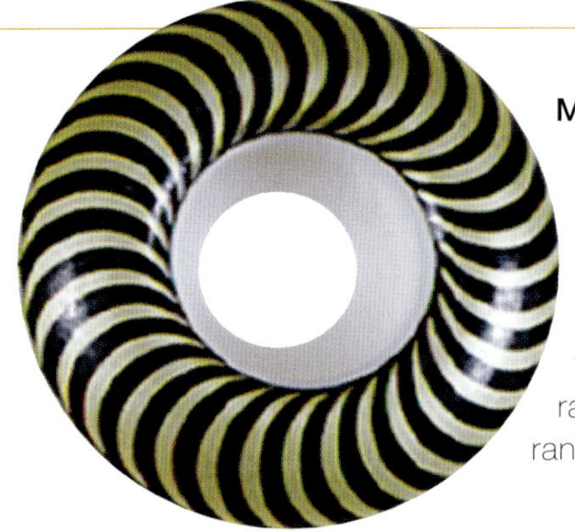

Miniramp, Pool, and Vert-Ramp Wheels

Wider and bigger wheels are preferred here. Ramps are paved, which means that rough terrain isn't an issue—so you want something that's smooth and fast. A bigger wheel has proved to maintain a faster speed than a smaller wheel. It's a matter of physics. (Dig it: Skateboarding is science, too.) The average wheel for skating ramps ranges from 55 to 60 mm with a durometer ranging from 97a to 101a.

All-Terrain Wheels

The average all-terrain wheel ranges from 54 to 58 mm with durometer range of 97a to 101a. These sizes meet the demands of most conditions. Again, if you're comfortable on what you ride, you can pretty much ride anything. Just go skate.

Cruiser Wheels

When choosing a cruiser wheel, you want something that's big and soft so that you can roll over almost anything—pizza boxes, broken glass, whatever. The best cruiser wheel size ranges from 58 to 65 mm with a durometer range of 80a to 90a. With this size wheel you don't have to worry about cracks or potholes, and you can roll superfast.

My Setup

Yo: As I mentioned before, this is all the stuff I ride. I recommend it—but remember, it's all about personal preference. Try a bunch of different setups before you find the one you prefer.

*Shorty's Muska 7.5-inch deck: $55
*Ghetto Child 52-mm wheels: $32
*Independent trucks: $45
*Shorty's Silverados ⅞-inch Allen nuts and bolts: $5
*Black Panthers bearings: $40
*Black Magic grip tape: $6
Total cost: $183

Not bad for a killer board that'll last you a long, long time. I bet you've spent more on Backstreet Boys CDs. But that chapter of your life is over.

FYI:

If you don't live near a skateboard shop, you can order a skate gear catalog from CCS (800-477-9283) or head to CCS.com to get all the goods.

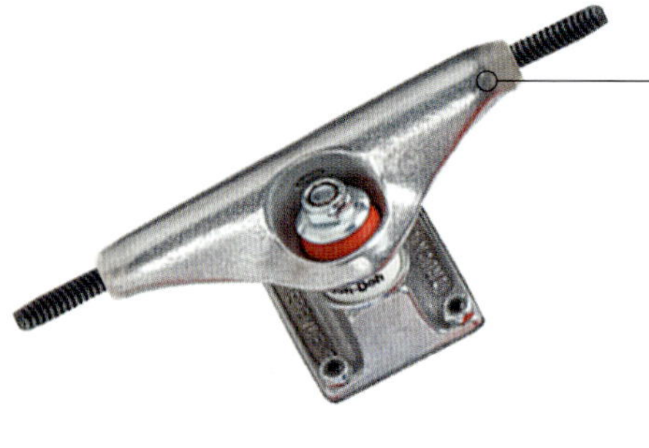

Trucks

the truck: The metal fastener that attaches your wheels to the board and allows you to turn.

the axle: The pin on which the pair of wheels revolves.

There is no specific truck for street, vert, or cruising. But the size truck you buy should fit your board. If you have a wider board, you want a wider truck. If you have bigger wheels, you want a taller truck. You do not want a truck that is wider than your board because if the ends stick out, you're going to trip over them. You also increase the chances of an "axle slip." This is when the axle comes loose from hitting the ground too many times—which causes one side of your truck to tighten up on the wheel and may stop your wheel from spinning. This in turn sends you flying into the street, which is no fun.

Again, as with all skateboard equipment, try out a bunch of different trucks before you find the one you like best. Some trucks are lighter than others, and some trucks turn better than others. Ask your local skate shop employee. No, wait, he won't answer. Ask a friend who has tried a lot of different trucks to recommend one. Independent is the brand I use; the total cost per set is about $45. They're light, and they turn really well.

Grip Tape

grip tape: A rough, sandpapery sheet of glue and finely ground gravel that helps your feet stay gripped to your board.

Black Magic is definitely the best brand of grip tape out there. It only costs six bucks. It has the perfect grit, sticks well to your board, and lasts longer than the other brands. Of course, some tapes have graphics, some have different colors, and some have die cuts—but keep in mind that these coloring processes affect the quality of the tape, and they don't grip as well. The question is: Do you want to look all stupid crazy, or do you want to stay on your board?

Bearings

bearings: Tiny metal balls that are inserted in your wheel to help the wheel spin.

the "abec" rating system: A system designed to rate bearings for the machining industry. It has nothing to do with the performance of bearings for skateboarding. IMPORTANT: Ignore somebody if they try to tell you that the "abec" rating system matters in any way. It doesn't, unless you drive a tractor or use a jackhammer.

Choosing the right bearing is very important. You want to choose a bearing that performs well and lasts long. Again, don't be fooled by the whole "abec" thing. A bearing that is an abec 9 can be just as good as a bearing that is an abec 3. It really depends on the quality of the brand. Unfortunately, the price of the bearing generally reflects its quality. The prices range anywhere from $15 to $45. My advice to you is to save up for some good ones, like **Black Panthers Bearings.** You don't want to have a board that sucks.

Riser Pads

riser pad: A soft pad that separates the truck from the board. The pad prevents your wheels from rubbing against your board and also helps prevent stress cracks that may occur from hard impacts.

shock pad: A more cushy riser pad, for tricks that are harder on your board.

Riser pads depend solely on the size of the setup you're riding. For example, if you're riding a 7.5-inch board with 50-mm wheels, you do not need a riser pad. I don't use one, so I can't really recommend one. Some skateboarders prefer to ride a shock pad, which will keep your mounting hardware tight and prevent stress cracks. If you're riding a wheel that is 55 mm or more, you might want to look into riser pads, as they help prevent "wheel bite." This is the term for what happens when your wheel accidentally rubs against your board and causes you to stop abruptly. (In other words, it's a nice way of saying you will get a concussion.) The bigger the wheel you ride, the wider riser pad you will need. They generally cost around $4.

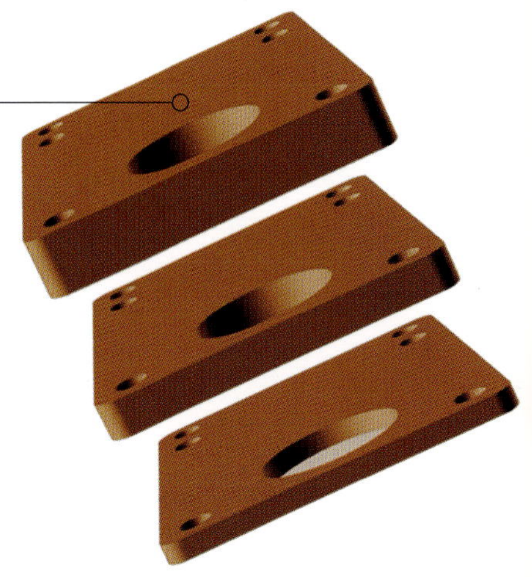

Hardware

Phillips head: A bolt with an x-shaped head.
Allen head: A bolt with a hexagonal head.

Hardware consists of eight bolts and eight nuts. There are different sizes— ⅞ inch, 1 inch, 1⅛ inch, 1¼ inch, and 1½ inch—all of which are available in either a Phillips head or an Allen head. Choosing the right size hardware depends on whether you ride riser pads or not. For example, if you don't ride riser pads, ⅞ inch or 1 inch is suggested. If you ride a ⅛ inch riser pad, you should ride 1 inch or 1⅛ inch. And so on. There are a lot of different hardware brands to choose from, and a lot of companies just buy stock hardware. But then there are companies like Shorty's who design their own hardware specifically for skateboarding. Shorty's makes a half-threaded bolt to be stronger and a smaller head to sink deeply into the board so the head doesn't stick out. They also make a brand of hardware that comes with two silver bolts—Silverados—so you can tell the nose of your board from the tail. The set costs around $5.

The Skate Shop

There is no other retail business in the free world that even compares to the skateboard shop.

It doesn't matter how much money you have or who you are. Even if you're an MC for the WuTang Clan, you will still be ignored. The skateboard shop employee is the laziest and rudest person in retail. But he has the best possible job. Here are some reasons why:

- Store hours start sometime after noon and end right when a customer shows up to buy something.
- You get to watch videos and read skateboard magazines all day.
- If you're tired, you get to take a nap.
- The ruder you are, the more respect you get.
- The #1 reason it's the best job: If you work at a cool enough shop, most companies will send you free products.

Customer Service

"Customer service" is a phrase that you will never hear in the skate shop. Even though the employees have the best jobs in the world, they would still rather be outside skateboarding than helping customers try on shoes. Who can blame them? It sucks for you, the customer, but that's where you have to go to get the gear. And it's a funny thing, too, because even though you can never get any help, you'll still keep coming back. It's guaranteed. Also guaranteed: The rudest skate shop is always the skateboarders' favorite. Sometimes it's even like going to a stand-up comedy show. The employees will dis you and clown on the clothes you're wearing and generally make you feel like The Mongo. Just watch your comebacks because if you've got a smart mouth, you might get a wheel thrown at your face.

Everything listed in this book. A skate shop is pretty much all-purpose. Some shops will feature a deck wall where you can actually pull down the deck you want to see. Other shops are too paranoid about theft; a sneaky skater can snag a deck off the wall while all the employees are playing craps. The paranoid shops keep their decks behind the counter. Unfortunately that's kind of a drag because sometimes it's really hard to find the shape you want—and when you ask to see several different decks, the employees can get very annoyed and often violent. Shoes will usually be displayed on a shoe wall where you can pick out what you want and request a size. As you can see in the photo, it's not always easy to actually see the shoe in your size. T-shirts and other clothing are usually cluttered together on a round rack, and you'll be lucky to find what you want. All the good stuff goes pretty fast. Accessories, wheels, videos, trucks, hardware, bearings, and stickers are kept in a glass display case. One piece of advice: If you ask the skate shop employee how much each sticker costs, they're going to get mad and ignore you for the rest of your shopping visit. Most stickers are a dollar, so just buy it and shut up.

Well, if you can convince an employee to help you, you're golden—but good luck. Sometimes you might not be able to find them at all. They're usually busy playing craps, using the bathroom, sleeping, or outside skating.

Here's a list of things to do while waiting to make a purchase:

- Check out the newest skate magazine or watch a video.
- Take money out of the cash register. That's a joke, of course! Ha, ha, ha!

cos

The Mongo's Guide to
safety
Gear

Name: Toan Nguyen
Age: 21
Hometown: Santa Barbara
Something you should know about Toan: He's a magician. He can pull a quarter out of your ear, and there won't be any wax on it. Amazing!
Credentials (Important for safety instruction): Gifted at the headspin. Performs insane magic tricks for Shorty's. Doesn't wear any of the safety gear pictured in these photos.

Okay, I know that safety gear looks cheesy. If you go to a skate park where they force you to wear pads, it can totally ruin your session. On the other hand, if you get into an accident and die, you can't skate anymore. Hopefully, there will be skate shops in the afterlife, but we can't be sure. They might not have the kind of graphic or board you like. Just be smart: try to protect yourself from bodily harm.

The Helmet

A helmet is used to butt your friends in the head. All right, seriously: most street skaters don't wear helmets unless they have overprotective moms. Generally you will see helmets at skate parks and vert ramps. If you're clumsy and trip a lot, you might want to wear a helmet. A skateboard helmet is also good for headspins.

Elbow Pads

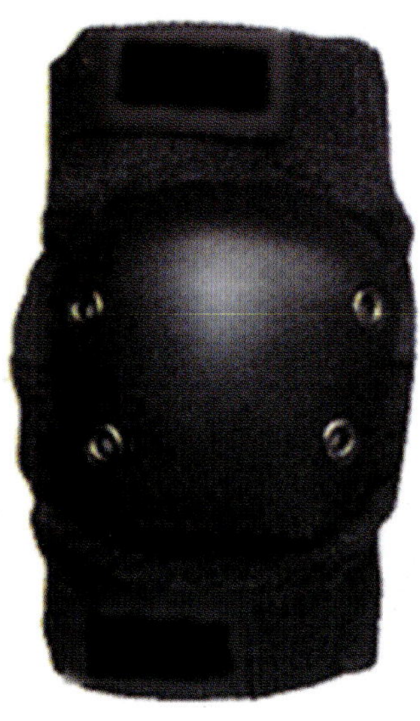

Elbow pads are used to prevent "swellbow." This is a medical term for a condition that arises when your elbow gets swollen. As in the case of the helmet, most street skaters don't wear elbow pads. They just don't feel very functional. If you want to impress the girls at school, you might want to wear them—you know, if the girls at your school dig that in-line-skate look. You should wear them when you're eating dinner, too, so you can put your elbows on the table. That way you can irritate your mom and be comfortable at the same time.

Knee Pads

Knee pads are used to run really fast and skid across the ground and floor on your knees. Most skateboarders don't wear these, either. It comes down to this: skateboarders just don't like wearing any pads. Period. (Well, unless they're pulling really, really insane tricks.) Too bad the rest of the world doesn't understand. Of course, you will occasionally see knee pads at skate parks and vert ramps—and I would probably recommend knee pads if you're skating vert because it might save those ankles from twisting when you're running down the ramp.

Wrist Guards

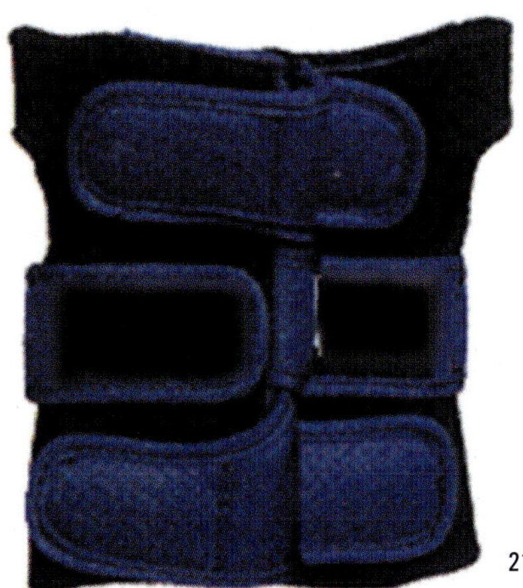

Wrist guards help keep your wrist from bending the wrong way. If you chill on watching Britney Spears and Jennifer Lopez videos, you won't need a wrist guard. Wrist guards, knee pads, black slacks, and an unbuttoned white T-shirt make a great costume for Halloween, particularly if you want to be Michael Jackson.

The Mongo's Guide to
being in
Style

The T2

This look originates from living across the street from my homeboy Tony Tieu (see page 71). I spend all of my time trying to copy the way he dresses. Sometimes when he leaves his house, I climb through the window and steal his clothes.

Hollywood

You know how the stars dress. You gotta look fly when you're in LA. If you're not wearing the right gear, then you better take yourself to Melrose. Oh yeah—don't forget the cellie.

Tech

This look is for the real skate freaks. It's all about having the lightest and most comfortable gear. You can see this type of look on So-Cal skate legends like Muska.

Rico

This is how my mom dresses me. Most skateboarders dress like this because they don't have the cash to look really dope.

Nor-Cal

It's cold up north of LA. Cold weather makes people mad. So when you want to slash through a skate park or just blast frontside airs all day, this is what you want to wear. Now get out of my way because these pants are tight and I'm pissed.

Tha SD

Where the ghetto meets the sea, yo. All the real gangstas represent from San Diego. And when you jus' chillin' and waking up around four in the afternoon, this the style you want to kick. All I gotta say, dog, is: "WEEEEESSST SIIIIIDE!"

Fro

This is the get-kicked-out-of-every-hotel, destroy-every-hotel-room, not-quite-a-rock-star look. It requires that you grow a lot of nappy hair, cut off your sleeves, and pull crooked grinds (see page 74) all day long.

Glam

Glam? Glam is dead, kid. This is the Oscar-the-Grouch, I-sleep-in-a-garbage-can look. In other words, it's what looks best when you puke on yourself. Daily routine for this getup: wake up, drink soda, puke, skate, drink more soda, puke, skate . . . Repeat as often as necessary.

setting up a
Skateboard

First things first. Put on your favorite Poison CD. (Personally, I prefer *Open Up and Say . . . Ahhhh!*) Then grab your dad's tools and let's rock and roll.

When laying down the grip tape, be sure to avoid air bubbles. Lay it slowly and carefully. Taking your time is key.

Massage the board. That's right. Show it some love. Wow, my muscles are getting really big. I guess it's because I have been eating all those muscle bars.

Setting Up A Board

Instructions by Judas

Name: Judas (last name unknown)

Age: 23

Hometown: LA

Personal history: Rumored to be raised by Poison roadies until he accidentally was abandoned in Detroit at the age of five. Later tagged along with Warrant and Cinderella until he eventually made his way back to California. At the age of fourteen, Judas moved in with the ex-girlfriend of Rikki Rocket (Poison's drummer and current animal rights activist)—where he discovered a skateboard. He quickly ditched the girl for his new love: skateboarding. Something you should know about Judas: Everything he learned was self-taught, so his methods may appear to be highly unusual.

Step 4.

Before cutting the sides off the grip, take your dad's favorite screwdriver and file around the edge. This will make it easier to cut off the excess grip.

Step 5.

This is where you cut off the excess grip. I prefer to use a saw but a razor blade will work too. Just be careful not to cut off a finger. Filing the edges down after this is recommended as well.

Step 6.

Put the bearings in the wheels. This part is hard. Sometimes I get so angry that I just hammer the stupid things until they go in. You might want to try a different method, like maybe running over the board with a car!

Step 7.

Go to track 8 on your Poison CD. You will need to hear "Every Rose Has Its Thorn" in order to finish setting up your board. Now tighten the axle nut but not so tight that your wheels can't spin freely.

Step 8.

First, attach your trucks to your board by placing the hardware through the holes. Second, mount your trucks to your board. Third, make sure that you tighten the nuts or you will be in big trouble. You're done—now grab your boom box and your Poison CD and go skate.

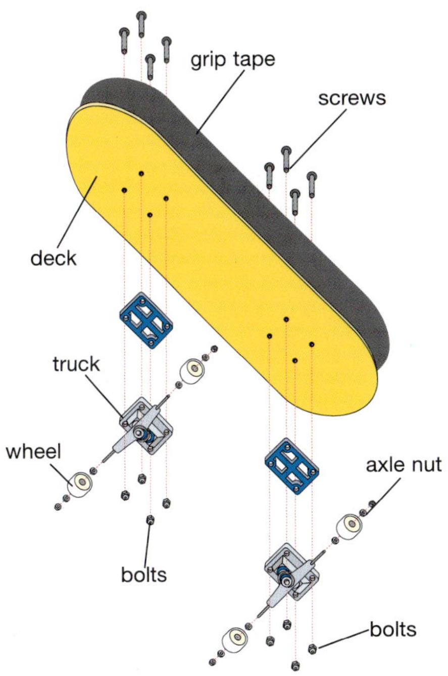

The Mongo's Guide to

LOVES AND HATES

HATES:
In-Line Skaters

The skateboarder's dislike of in-line skaters originated the moment people started strapping those
silly fruit boots to their feet. Nobody really knows
why. But I do know this: in-line skaters are pretty
annoying creatures. They're like cockroaches. You
think you tripped the last one, then—yikes!—there's
another one grinding right behind him. They infest
all the skate parks and skate spots and leave slimy
overwaxed trails in their wake.

We don't promote tripping and pushing them,
but that's not a bad idea if you thought it up on your
own. Besides, most of them are so padded up, they
won't feel a thing. The point is, they should always
look where they're going.

HATES:
Razor Scooters

Scooters. Where did those awful things come from? One day you're having a great time at the skate park, pulling all these killer tricks—and the next it's infested with scooters. Okay, I don't really hate the scooters, but I don't particularly care for the people who ride them. There's no learning process. It's just (a) buy a scooter, (b) ride a scooter, and (c) get in everybody's way with a scooter. But hey, if you're okay with kicking it like the momma's boy next door, then feel free. Rico Suave does. That's why we throw him in the trash a lot. Just understand the consequences. Once you go scooter, you enter a terrible world from which there may be no turning back.

HATES:
Nothing Else, Really

Skateboarders are positive. We're not a bunch of haters. So why do we have such a bad reputation? It doesn't make sense. Besides in-line skates and scooters, I can't really think of anything else that we hate. Okay, sometimes our friends annoy us. That's why we have to beat them down every now and then. Personally, I prefer the frying-pan beat-down method, as pictured in this photograph. What you want to do is stand on a kitchen sink or refrigerator, wait for your friend to walk through the doorway, then jump on his back and smack him over the head. And if another friend is available, kindly ask him to join the fun and punch your victim in the stomach. Not that we advocate violence.

Loves: *music*

Skateboarders are human beings, too—so like all human beings, they listen to all kinds of music. Yes, they even have different tastes. Just like regular people. So instead of telling you what kind of music to listen to, we'll throw out a couple of suggestions. Feel free to ignore all of them. Music is about expression, about being an individual, about the sound track to your life. Don't let people try to ram their music down your throat. It's like skateboarding. No wonder most skateboarders have really kicking sound systems.

Hip-Hop

Definitely the most popular music among skateboarders today. Skateboarding and hip-hop have a lot in common. Both blew up in the eighties and nineties. Both are about personal expression, about representing your 'hood and style. Hip-hop can pump you up and put mad flavor in your flow. The beats can also create a sound track to skateboarding. Every time that phat beat drops, land that trick.

Here are some of our favorite picks: Run DMC, Boogie Down Productions, Public Enemy, Cypress Hill, Tribe Called Quest, De La Soul, Beastie Boys, N.W.A., Hieroglyphics, Eric B. & Rakim, Jungle Brothers, WuTang Clan, Common, Mos Def, Talib Kweli, Freestyle Fellowship, Blackalicious, Biz Markie, Digable Planets, Gang Starr, Ultra Magnetic MCs, Jeru the Damaja, Main Source, Outkast, Organized Confusion, Pharcyde, Pete Rock and C.L. Smooth, LL Cool J, Grandmaster Flash, Sugar Hill Gang, Afrikaa Bambataa, The Roots, EPMD, Black Sheep, Black Moon, Too Short, Company Flow, and the list could go on and on, but we don't have enough space.

A good CD to burn if you're skating vert ramps:

"Work"—Gang Starr
"Oakland Blackouts"—Hieroglyphics
"Your Momma"—Pharcyde
"Me and The Biz"—Masta Ace
"Jane"—EPMD
"Just Another Day"—Too Short
"Straight Outta Compton"—N.W.A.
"Hey Ladies"—Beastie Boys
"Ego Trippin"—De La Soul
"Scenario"—Tribe Called Quest
"Just a Ho"—Presidio Players

Punk

Skateboarders have listened to punk probably longer than any other type of music. That's because punks are truly the founding fathers of skateboarding as it's known today. The So-Cal punks in particular. It's as if George Washington and his crew had lived in southern California in the seventies, and they all had spiky hair and smelly leather jackets. Okay, not really. But punks were among the first skaters to pull the really insane tricks. Their music is fast and filled with rebellion, and it was born in the streets—just like skateboarding. 'Cause sometimes you just have to say screw everything and do it your way. That's why punk makes you want to skate as fast as possible and kickflip fourteen stairs (see page 63).

The bands we like: Sex Pistols, Black Flag, Fear, Adolescents, 7 Seconds, Murphy's Law, Youth Brigade, The Germs, Minor Threat, Bad Brains, Buzzcocks, Misfits, Circle Jerks, Butthole Surfers, Dead Kennedys, Day Glo Abortions, DRI, Suicidal Tendencies, Bad Religion, NOFX, Fugazi, Agent Orange, TSOL, The Exploited, Crass. Again, the list could go on and on, but this should help you on your way to becoming an anarchist.

A good CD to burn if you want to try very dangerous tricks:

"Kill the Poor"—Dead Kennedys
Anything off Hairway to Steven—Butthole Surfers
"Sub-Mission"—Sex Pistols
"Hide the Hamster"—Day Glo Abortions
"99 Red Balloons"—7 Seconds
"Crucial Bar-B-Q"—Murphy's Law
"Six Pack"—Black Flag
"Institutionalized"—Suicidal Tendencies

(By this time you'll be dead, so there's really no point in continuing.)

Jazz

Why is jazz like skateboarding? Because it's raw. Because it can be mellow or hard-edge. Because it has a massive improvisational element. Because there's so much style, and because it's art. You have to practice hours and hours a day; you have to master the fundamentals before you can really play—just like you have to master ollies before you can even think about pulling a 360 kickflip (see page 104). Almost all contemporary music can be traced to jazz: rock, hip-hop, soul, funk . . . the list goes on.

Some jazz greats to check out: Herbie Hancock, Ella Fitzgerald, Louis Armstrong, Billie Holiday, Miles Davis, John Coltrane, Charlie Parker, Charles Mingus, Dave Brubeck, Billy Cobham, Sarah Vaughan, Count Basie, and Duke Ellington. Much respect to all those missing here; you know who you are.

If you want to dig jazz while riding your cruiser board, burn this CD:

"A Love Supreme"—John Coltrane
"Donna Lee"—Charlie Parker & Dizzy Gillespie
"Hang Up Your Hang-Ups"—Herbie Hancock
"Take 5"—Dave Brubeck
"The Red Baron"—Billy Cobham
"All Blues"—Miles Davis
"Satin Doll"—Duke Ellington
"Let's Call the Whole Thing Off"—Louis Armstrong & Ella Fitzgerald

Metal

As we all know, metal is loud and causes jocks to fight. But for skateboarders, it might just make you skate really fast. While punk works on your mind and makes you think deep thoughts about stuff like politics, metal goes straight for your adrenaline. It makes you stupid. Which is good. (Occasionally.) You can't control yourself. You have to ollie the biggest gap. But be careful 'cause you might break a few bones and bang your head. Here's a list of some kick-ass metal groups: Slayer, Metallica, Judas Priest, Sepultura, Anthrax, Motorhead, Guns N' Roses, Pantera . . . Okay, that's enough metal. Too much might cause your skull to explode.

A good CD to burn if you want to skate down very steep hills:

"Angel of Death"—Slayer
"Piece by Piece"—Slayer
"Necrophobic"—Slayer
"Altar of Sacrifice"—Slayer
"Jesus Saves"—Slayer
"Criminally Insane"—Slayer
"Reborn"—Slayer
"Epidemic"—Slayer
"Back in Black"—AC/DC

Funk and Soul

Yeah, that's right, sometimes skaters like to slow down and show off our sensitive sides. Whether we're chilling with the ladies or sipping some malt liquor (grape juice if you're under twenty-one), we gotta get a groove on every once in a while. Maybe some skateboarders don't listen to funk and soul. But I'm a skater, and I do. So check it: Rick James, Parliament Funkadelic, Kool & the Gang, The Meters, James Brown, B.T. Express, Chocolate Milk, Earth Wind & Fire, Al Green, Isaac Hayes, Curtis Mayfield, SOUL, Bill Withers, and, of course, Stevie Wonder.

A good CD to burn when you've hung up your board for the day, you've just put on your fly white polyester suit, and you're having one of your honeys over for a romantic candlelight dinner:

"Give Up the Funk"—Parliament Funkadelic
"Give It to Me, Baby"—Rick James
Anything off Songs in the Key of Life—Stevie Wonder
"Rubberband"—The Meters
"Shaft"—Isaac Hayes
"Superfly"—Curtis Mayfield
"Sing a Song"—Earth Wind & Fire
"Hollywood Swinging"—Kool & the Gang
"All Night Long"—Mary Jane Girls
"Sex Machine"—James Brown

Country

There are only two country musicians worth listening to (I mean looking at): Shania Twain and Faith Hill. Leave the rest for the cowboys. Country makes you skateboard worse.

Pop

Don't worry about pop music. Leave that stuff for your little sister.

We could continue, but then we'd have to write another book. Other types of music that aren't listed that you might want to check out are drum 'n' bass, jungle, house, blues, R&B, classical, Latin, emo, classic rock, alternative rock . . . All right, forget it. Just find what you like and use it to get yourself hyped, to learn tricks, to skate well. And if you can't think of anything besides a skateboard accessory as a gift for one of your homies, remember these lists.

Here's what Judas and I listen to when we skate:

The "I'm-the-Mack-So-Step-Back" Collection
"93 'Til Infinity"—Souls of Mischief
"Mistadobalina"—Del Tha Funkee Homosapien
"I Ain't No Joke"—Eric B. & Rakim
"Jazz"—Tribe Called Quest
"Radio"—LL Cool J
"Get in Where You Fit In"—Too Short
"Bombs over Baghdad"—Outkast
"Accepted Eclectic"—Aceyalone
"A to G"—Blackalicious
"I Was Drunk"—Presidio Players
"Passing Me By"—Pharcyde
"JBs Coming Through"—Jungle Brothers
"Hard Times"—Run DMC
"C.R.E.A.M."—Wu Tang Clan
"Eternalists"—Talib Kweli

The Judas Frying-Pan Beat-Down Mix
"Every Rose Has Its Thorn"—Poison
"Sweet Child o' Mine"—Guns N' Roses
"Who's That Girl"—Madonna
"Uncle Tom's Cabin"—Warrant
"18 and Life"—Skid Row
"Don't Know What You Got"—Cinderella
"Dr. Feelgood"—Motley Crue

Ah, the Skateboard Diet. As I might have mentioned before, skateboarders are also human beings. So of course they require food. As a skateboarder, you will, too. You need to follow a strict diet of sugar, fat, and grease. These three essential food groups are the keys to health and successful skateboarding. If you're over eighteen, caffeine is highly recommended as well.

Breakfast

Start off each morning with a glass of soda. Personally, I like **Buzz.** But you don't want to drink it straight. Add as much sugar as possible to the glass, preferably one cup. Stir it around. If you're over eighteen, mix it with a cup of coffee. Drink it! Mmm-mmm. Wasn't that tasty? Now you're ready for the main course. Grab the ice cream out of the freezer and scoop some out into a bowl. Any brand will do, so long as it's not low fat. Pour one cup of sugar on top of that (good!) and eat it with a cookie. I prefer **Oreo Double Stuf.** Go skate for a while. Nothing will stop you! (Warning: Side effects may include dizziness, euphoria, and occasional puking. Don't worry. That's completely natural.)

Lunch

When lunchtime rolls around, you'll need another power boost. And nothing has more energy than dog food. Haven't you ever seen how happy and energetic dogs are? They owe it all to their diet. If you're under twelve, I recommend **Purina Puppy Chow** and **Beggin' Strips**—but remember, like everything else in skateboarding, it's all a matter of personal preference. Maybe you'd rather go with **Alpo.** That's fine. Try a bunch of different brands before you find the one you like. If you're over twelve, I recommend **Purina Dog Chow.** Pour a little milk in there, just like cereal.

Okay. You don't actually believe that we want you to scarf down dog food, do you? (Otherwise, you might end up looking like the dude in this photo.) That's sick. Here's what you should *really* eat for lunch:

- •1 bag potato chips (whichever brand has the most fat)
- •1 liter soda (again, **Buzz**)
- •1 large pizza (with anchovies and extra cheese)

Now go skate.

Dinner

Some say that dinner is the most important meal of the day. Some say breakfast. The point is, they're all important. And after a tough day of skateboarding, you want to reward yourself. Here's what I recommend:

- •1 gallon of milk. If you're feeling brave, a gallon of half-and-half.
- •1 bag of cookies (**Double Stuf,** the clear choice)

Note: Your mom may have a problem with this diet. If she does, ignore her.

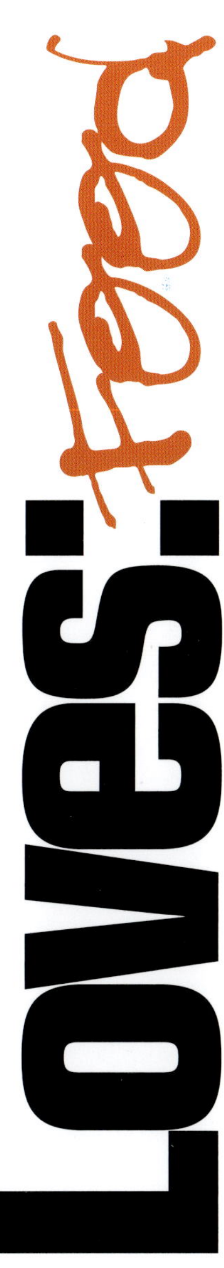

Watching Skateboard Videos

Skateboard videos are not only an excellent source of entertainment, but many also document the greatest moments in skateboarding history. So I guess you can say that they are educational as well. Here's a list of some the greatest skateboard videos of all time, presented chronologically—from Old School to New School. You should study them. I'll test you later. We have rated them using the universal "board" system (see below). But all the films listed are excellent in their own right. This list doesn't deal with the crappy videos.

+I see God.

Watch until the tape burns out.

Can't stop rewinding

Good, but would be better if *Baywatch* chicks played some minor role

Mommy, do I really have to watch this?

Promotional video for razor scooters

Future Primitive—Powell Peralta © 1985
The Bones Brigade crew taking charge.
Streets of Fire—Santa Cruz © 1985
The streets are on fire in this one.
Animal Chin—Powell Peralta © 1986
Kind of like eight-minute abs. Learn skateboard morning exercises in eight minutes.
Curb Dogs © 1987
Rock tha curbs, dog!
Public Domain—Powell Peralta © 1988
Check out skaters Ray Barbee and Cab wearing suspenders. Isn't that cool?
Shackle Me Not—HStreet © 1988
Some of the pros you know so well today as the kids they used to be.
Hokus Pokus—HStreet © 1989
Do you believe in magic? You will after you see this.
Hai Karate—Santa Cruz © 1990
Two words: Hai yah!
Video Days—Blind © 1991
Too much to say about this video; just check it out.

A Soldier's Story—Life © 1991
All I have to say is: Sean Sheffey.
Tim & Henry's Pack of Lies—Blind © 1992
Henry Sanchez and Tim Gavin show raw street skateboarding skills and blow your mind.
Questionable—Plan B © 1992
Your head will spin like that girl's in *The Exorcist*.

Loves:

Falling Down—101 © 1993
I fall down every once in a while, too.

Super Conductor Super Collider—Foundation © 1993
The best Foundation team ever: Steve Olson, Frank Hirata, Heath Kirchart, Steve Berra, and Ronnie Creager wreck shop.

Rolling Thunder—Foundation © 1995
Part deux. Again, the Foundation team delivers another insane collection.

Mouse—Girl © 1996
Skaters Koston and Carroll . . . what the hell else do I have to say?

Welcome to Hell—Toy Machine © 1996
Jamie Thomas pushes skateboarding to another level by ollieing everything in sight.

Fulfill the Dream—Shorty's © 1998
The first Shorty's Skateboard Team video. Innovation, that's all I gotta say. Videos just ain't been the same since, and neither has skateboarding.

The End—Birdhouse © 1998
The first 16-mm skateboard video. A lot of skits. You'll laugh your ass off. Definitely one of the most entertaining videos of all time.

Feedback—Transworld © 1999
Ty Evans creates a piece of art with a skateboarding video. Parts with skateboard legends Muska, Reynolds, and more.

Anthology—Transworld © 2000
A behind-the-scenes of skateboarding videos. After watching it, you'll think twice before you talk trash on certain pro skateboarders.

Menikmati—ES Shoes © 2001
Damn! These guys pull insane tricks for a shoe company?

Playing Video Games

When you're not skateboarding and you want to bust out with tricks that you've only dreamed about doing, play **Tony Hawk Pro Skater**. I'm sure there are other great games out there, but in my opinion **Tony Hawk Pro Skater** is the best skateboard game in the history of mankind. Another good one is **720**. Then there are all the rest of the video games—most of which have nothing to do with skateboarding—and those are all pretty good, too. Especially if your mom took your board away.

Pushing

How to Push

Pushing is the driving force of a skateboard. If you don't push, you're not getting any-where—unless you're on a steep hill or you tic-tac (see below). We encourage you to push with your back foot. The reasoning behind this is simple. Pushing with your front foot is straight-up stupid. It's bad for tricks; it messes with your balance; it's ill and it has no style. Let's just put it this way: Nobody will ever sponsor you if you push mongo.

History of the Mongo Push

The origins of the mongo push are unknown to man, lost in the dim mists of time. There have been rumors, though. Some say that your mom may have been one of the first to have pushed mongo, but there's no hard evidence to prove this accusation. In any event, throughout history, mongo pushers have always been criticized by their wiser peers. To avoid backlash and humiliation, some have mended their ways and learned to push with their back foot. They have all gone on to greatness.

The Present

Despite the efforts of the wise, the incidence of mongo is still rising at an alarming rate. Skate parks and streets are being overrun by these wrong-footed skateboarders. The sit-uation is nearly out of control. It must be stopped immediately before it's too late. But what can we do to help our more ignorant peers? How can we help these skateboarders move on to ever more sick tricks? How can we put style back into the skateboarding youth of today?

The Solution

You must help them. Yes, you must train them, like the dogs they are. And in order to do so, you must employ the following steps. Remember, by correcting mongo, you are sav-ing the future of skateboarding.

1. Make fun of your friends when you see them pushing mongo. History has taught us that nothing works better at correcting bad habits than peer pressure. (Example: "Hey, butt-wipe, learn how to push," or, "Hey, did your mom teach you how to push?")
2. Iron an antimongo logo onto one of their T-shirts.
3. Show them a skateboard video. Point out that all the pros in the video are pushing with their back foot, so they must be doing something right.
4. Take them to antimongo meetings. If peer pressure doesn't work, lend them support. Let them know that it will be a rough path, but it will all work out in the end.

tic-tac (TIK-TAK) *v.* To walk with your board by pushing down on the tail while simultane-ously lifting your nose and kicking it forward—then switching feet and kicking your tail for-ward, step by step. Makes a lot of noise.

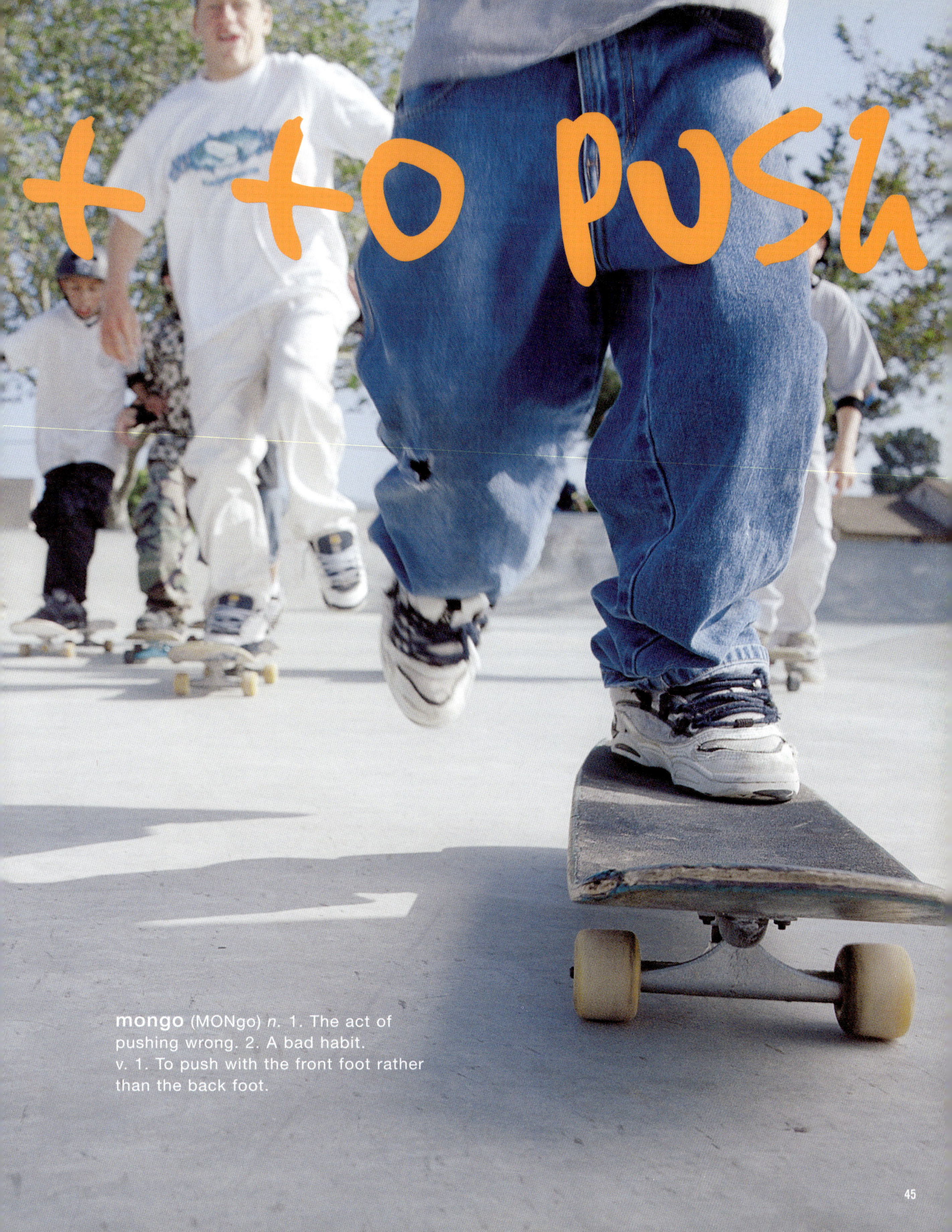

mongo (MONgo) *n.* 1. The act of
pushing wrong. 2. A bad habit.
v. 1. To push with the front foot rather
than the back foot.

Church of Skatan
CHILD
Shorty's
CHILD

The Mongo's Guide to
beginner
Tricks

Still Shot Skater:
Jake Stewart
Jake Stewart is from the Great White North. That's Canada to you. Jake is one of the few skateboarders who has the capability to pop ollies higher than you can believe.

The Ollie

ollie
(OL-lee) n. the act of jumping into the air on your board. v. To make your board jump off the ground.
•Skate legend Alan Gelfand invented the ollie in 1977.
•The ollie is the trick. Learn it.
•If you can't ollie, you can't skate.
• Like the origins of the mongo push, the origins of the word ollie have long since been lost. Maybe someday a historian will uncover this secret.

Remember: Start your ollies small. Slowly work your way up to bigger obstacles and gaps. Stacy's an expert. That's why he's allowed to ollie train tracks.

Place your front foot about four to six inches behind your front bolts. Your back foot should be right on the tail.

You want to pop your ollie by pushing down on your tail. Do this right before you get to the obstacle.

Slide your front foot toward the nose of your board.

Move your weight to the front of your board until it's completely level.

Keep your knees bent and your board level.

You must keep your board level as you start preparing to land.

Begin extending your legs so that you can absorb the impact of the ollie. Keep your weight centered. Absorb the shock and ride away.

Sequence Skater:
Stacy Lowery
Skills: Has the most amazing pop.
Vital stats: Twenty-five years old. Represents tha LBC (Long Beach, fool!)—just like Snoop Dogg. Can pretty much ollie over anything you can't.
Board Sponsor: Santa Cruz.

step 1.

Make sure you're comfortable with regular ollies first. Unlike the ollie, speed is needed because that's what helps the rotation.

step 2.

Once you figure out your perfect speed, bend your knees and ollie.

step 3.

As you leave the ground and your foot starts sliding toward the nose, start turning your body frontside.

step 4.

Continue to rotate your ollie. An important part of this trick is the speed of your rotation: the longer the ollie, the slower the 180.

step 5.

Start preparing to land. At this point you should have almost completed your rotation. Stay straight and land flat. You must also be ready to start bending your knees.

step 6.

Start bending your knees to absorb impact. Be ready to roll fakie. Roll away. You're done.

step 7.

Now do it again.

Sequence Skater:
Jason Phillips

Skills: Can pull every trick in this book.
Vital stats: Old School Santa Barbara pro. He's been ripping since back in the Powell Skate Zone days (translation: early nineties, see page 40) and is still breaking it off.

•Rico Suave frontside 180'd these stairs.
•The next day he came back and frontside 360'd these stairs on his scooter.
•The day after that, we got him with the frying-pan beat down.

Frontside 180 Ollie

frontside (FRONT-sid) *adj.* Toward the nose of your board. If you're regular (right footed), frontside is toward your left foot. If you're goofy (left footed), frontside toward your right foot.

fakie (FA-kee) *adv.* backward. (See step 6.)

frontside 180 ollie (FRONT-sid WUN-AT-ee OL-lee) *n.* The act of pulling an ollie while rotating 180 degrees frontside

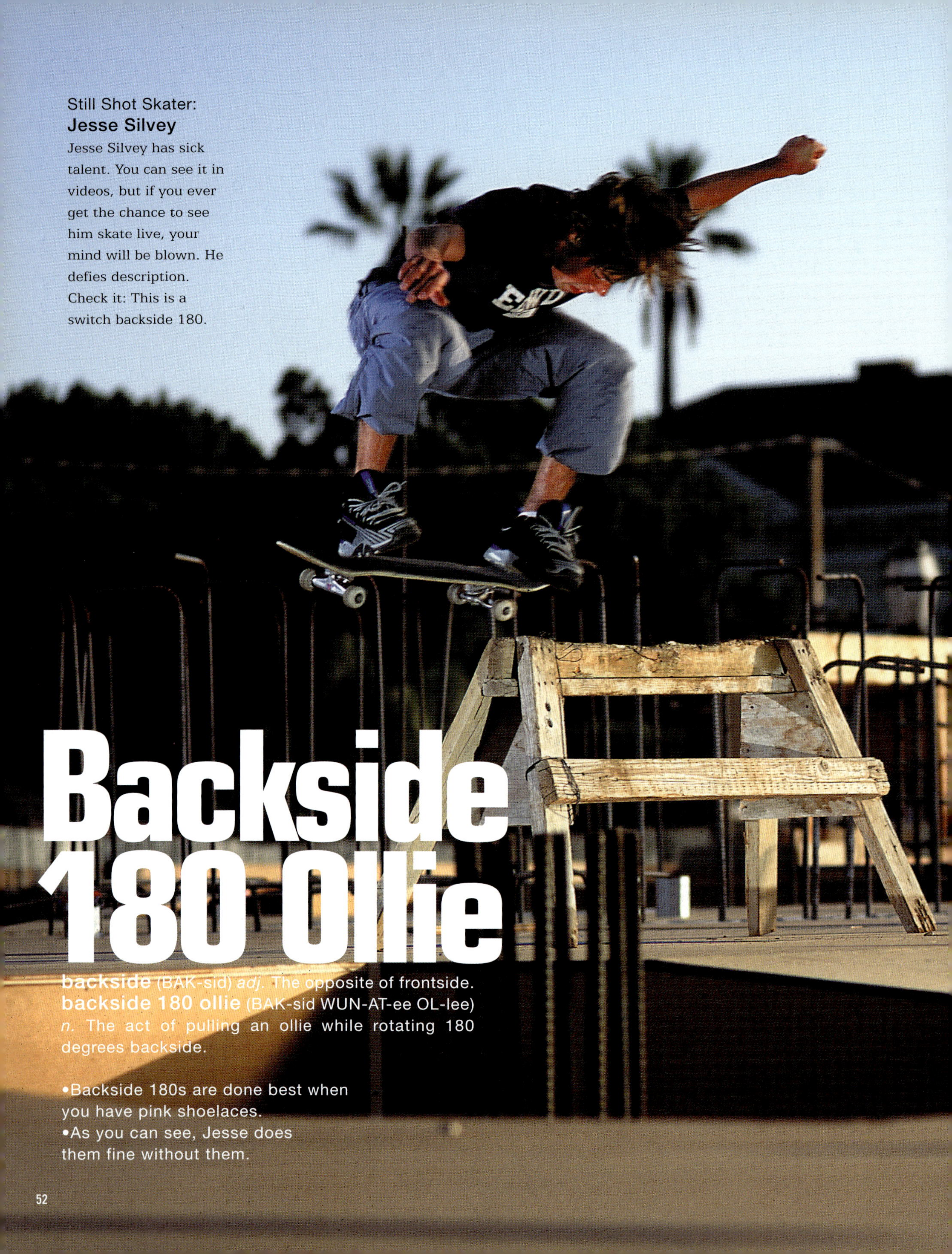

Still Shot Skater:
Jesse Silvey

Jesse Silvey has sick talent. You can see it in videos, but if you ever get the chance to see him skate live, your mind will be blown. He defies description. Check it: This is a switch backside 180.

Backside 180 Ollie

backside (BAK-sid) *adj.* The opposite of frontside.
backside 180 ollie (BAK-sid WUN-AT-ee OL-lee) *n.* The act of pulling an ollie while rotating 180 degrees backside.

•Backside 180s are done best when you have pink shoelaces.
•As you can see, Jesse does them fine without them.

step 1.

Gain a comfortable speed (not too slow). Place your foot in standard ollie position.

step 2.

Ollie.

step 3.

Once you take off, immediately start your backside rotation.

step 4.

If you're doing a backside 180 ollie over something big, rotate slowly; if over something small, rotate a little faster.

step 5.

Rotate your body at the same speed as your board

step 6.

Land flat on all four wheels at the same time.

step 7.

Bend your knees to absorb the shock of the ollie.

step 8.

You'll land fakie, so be ready to roll with it. If not, put on a bandage and try again.

Sequence Skater:

Damian Bravo

Skills: All.

Vital stats: Straight out of Alaska—which is great for dog sledding but not so good for skateboarding. During the winter the sun only comes out for about three or four hours, and temperatures generally hover around fifteen degrees Farenheit. So Damian moved. He currently lives and skates too damn well in Santa Barbara.

Warning: Don't be fooled by how easy he makes this trick look.

step 1.
Get used to rolling around fakie. Practice fakie ollies and have your 180 ollies down.

step 2.
Position your feet as you would for a 180 ollie. Bend your knees slightly.

step 3.
Fakie ollie. Once you pop that tail, start your rotation immediately. As you're rotating, move your weight forward so you even out. Rotate your body at the same speed as your board. Keep your feet over the bolts.

step 4.
Now get ready to land. You're going to want to start bending your knees to absorb the impact.

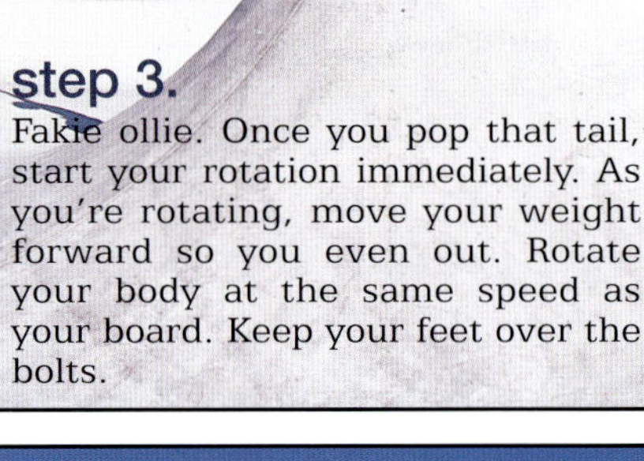

step 5.
Bend your knees and land flat. Keep bending those knees. Up and down, up and down. Ben practices Jazzercise with his mom so he can bend his knees down this far. You might want to do the same.

step 6.
Land that puppy clean and roll away.

Still Shot Skater:
Levi Marvin
Levi Marvin
is another
underground
Santa Barbara
ripper. He's all
about raw talent.

Half Cab

half cab (HAFF CAB) n. A fakie frontside or
backside 180 ollie.

•Invented and named by Steve "Cab" Caballero.
•Sometimes I tell people about the time I was
filmed frontside half cabbing over a semi truck.
Unfortunately, I lost the tape.
•No, seriously. I'm not fronting. I just lost it.

step 1.

Place your front foot just behind your front bolts.

step 2.

Ollie and at the same time use your back foot to shove your board around 180 degrees so that your tail is now your nose. The harder you shove the board, the faster it will rotate. Find the speed that's most comfortable for you.

step 3.

Keep your eyes on your board as it rotates. Once it has rotated a full 180 degrees, use your front foot to stop the rotation.

step 4.

Catch your board.

step 5.

Bend your knees slightly and land.

step 6.

Roll away with style. Then make a left and go get a soda. Pop shove-its make you thirsty.

Still Shot Skater:
Joey Pulsifer
Joey Pulsifer had some sick parts in the older Church of Skatan videos. You should see him skate now, though. He's even better.

Pop shove-it

pop shove-it (POP SHUV-it) *n.* The act of rotating your board 180 degrees as you pop an ollie.

- Learn pop shove-its really well.
- The pop shove-it is the key to the harder tricks.
- People mess up on this trick all the time because it looks too easy.

Ollie.

Shift your weight back, moving your feet toward your tail.

Your back foot should be past the back truck bolts; your front foot should be directly over the front bolts.

Keep your balance.

If your wheels or nose touch, try again.

Make sure you have a good amount of speed. Land flat on all four wheels and roll away.

Sequence Skater:
Brandon Turner

Skills: natural ability with smooth style.
Vital stats: Eighteen years old. A prodigy from Clairmont, California. One of those kids who was a natural and has been an insane skater since he was really little.
Board Sponsor: Shorty's

Manual

manual (MANuel) *n.* The act of balancing on your front trucks and wheels only.

nose manual (NOZ MANuel) *n.* The act of balancing on your back trucks and wheels only.

- Sometimes called "wheelies."
- Manuals and nose manuals are all about balance.
- Watch *The Karate Kid.* Learn how to do that balancing thing on the pole.
- Invented by a guy named Manuel, but no one knew how to spell his name.

Nose Manual

Ollie.

Shift your weight forward, moving your front foot toward your nose.

Your front foot should be past the front truck bolts; your back foot should be directly over the back bolts.

Keep your balance.

Same as the manual: if your wheels or nose touch, try again.

Make sure you have a good amount of speed. Land flat on all four wheels and roll away.

step 1.

Place your front foot on the nose of your board and the back foot slightly in front of the back truck.

step 2.

Push down on your nose while lifting weight off your back foot, which should cause your board to pop.

step 3.

Slide your back foot toward your tail, as you would for an ollie.

step 4.

As soon as you stop your tail from rising, start bringing your front foot to meet the level of your back foot.

step 5.

Your front foot should be over the front bolts, and your back foot should be by your tail.

step 6.

Keep your knees slightly bent to absorb the shock of landing.

step 7.

Maintain your balance so that you complete your landing.

step 8.

Continue bending your knees and maintaining your balance. Roll away with complete style.

Sequence Skater:
Mark Appleyard

Skills: Blowing your mind.
Vital stats: Appleyard came out of nowhere (actually, just Canada). Later moved out to Huntington, California.
Board Sponsor: Flip.

Nollie

nollie (NOLlee) *n.* The act of pulling an ollie off the nose of your board with your front foot.

•Nollies were invented back in 1947 in New Mexico, when the human race first came into contact with aliens. One of the aliens pulled a nollie, then was frozen indefinitely for DNA testing.

•It was very sad.

•Luckily somebody saw the aforementioned nollie, so it was one of the only secrets that ever made it out of Area 51.

•If you want to see the perfect nollie, check out pro Paulo Diaz. No, he's never spent time in New Mexico.

Still Shot Skater:
Brian Hoard
Brian Hoard is currently skateboarding for Deca; check out his part in the Deca promo video. He represents Temecula, California.

Place your feet in an ollie position. Your front foot should be a bit more toward the heel edge of your board and your back foot should be on the tail. You should feel like you're slightly on your toes, not flat-footed.

Now, as you ollie, kick out your front foot—slightly toward your heel edge. Don't kick down.

As you watch your board flip over (from rail to rail, not end to end) be prepared to land on it. Ideally you want to catch the board with the bottom of your feet before you land on the ground.

Land with your feet over the bolts and ride away. A big part of this trick is a clean ollie.

Important note: Check out that sidewalk. *That's* ghetto.

Now blast some Snoop Dogg, cowboy, 'cause corn mullets are in!

Sequence Skater:
Peter Smolik

Skills: Innovation. He's the kind of guy who combines tricks in ways you can't even imagine.

Vital stats: Seems like he came out of nowhere. Actually, straight outta Clairmont. Age is unknown. Made jaws drop during his part in Shorty's *Fulfill the Dream* (see page 41). Sports the corn mullet.

Still Shot Skater:
Eric Bork

Eric Bork is straight out of Ventura, California, and is currently skating for Santa Cruz. This photo was not doctored. Another guy you have to see in person to believe.

Kickflip

kickflip (KIK·flip) *n.* The act of flipping your board toward you during an ollie.

- There are two styles of kickflips: the Mob flip and the Penny flip. The Mob flip is rougher; the Penny flip is smoother.
- Check out Baker 2G to see the Mob flip.
- Check out Tom Penny for straight style. In case you hadn't guessed, the Penny flip is named after him.
- If you know Andrew Reynolds, get him to teach you this trick.

Heelflip

heelflip (HEEL-flip) *n.* The act of flipping your board with your heel during an ollie.

- Has nothing to do with that brand of Heely's shoes, which also share the name of this trick. Whew.
- Sometimes you just gotta put the hammer down and strike thunder like Thor.

step 1.

First, go get a prettyboy, eighties-style haircut like Carlos here.

step 2.

Next, go find an obstacle. Get some speed and put your foot in heelflip position.

step 3.

Ollie. As you ollie, kick your front foot straight toward the nose. Kick it slightly to the toe edge of your board as well.

step 4.

Your board should spin toward your toe edge. Once you see that Black Magic grip, land that mutha.

step 5.

Catch your board over the bolts. Remember: When you flip it, stay over your board. Stay centered.

step 6.

Keep your knees slightly bent.

step 7.

Roll away clean.

step 8.

Now go shave your head.

Sequence Skater:

Carlos Juarez

Skills: Imitating Morrissey (former angst-ridden lead singer of The Smiths).

Vital stats: Another Santa Barbara fool. He gets pumped listening to such eighties bands as the Smiths and Echo & the Bunnymen.

Important note: No, it's not worth checking out those bands.

Approach the obstacle from a parallel position.

Work up a good amount of speed and ollie.

Get your back truck above the object and land back truck first.

Sequence Skater:
Chad Muska
Skills: Too lengthy to describe here
Vital stats: Twenty-four years old but has already been a legend for years. One of the most famous skaters out there. Sick. Has his own line of shoes, clothing, decks and wheels. Nobody represents harder for southern California.
Board Sponsor:
Shorty's

Bend your knees and lock into your grind. Bending your knees will help you keep your balance.

Lift up your front truck slightly and prepare to come off of your grind. Extend your legs, but be ready to bend them when you land.

Land flat. Bend your knees to absorb the impact. Roll away. Now go say "what's up" to your homies.

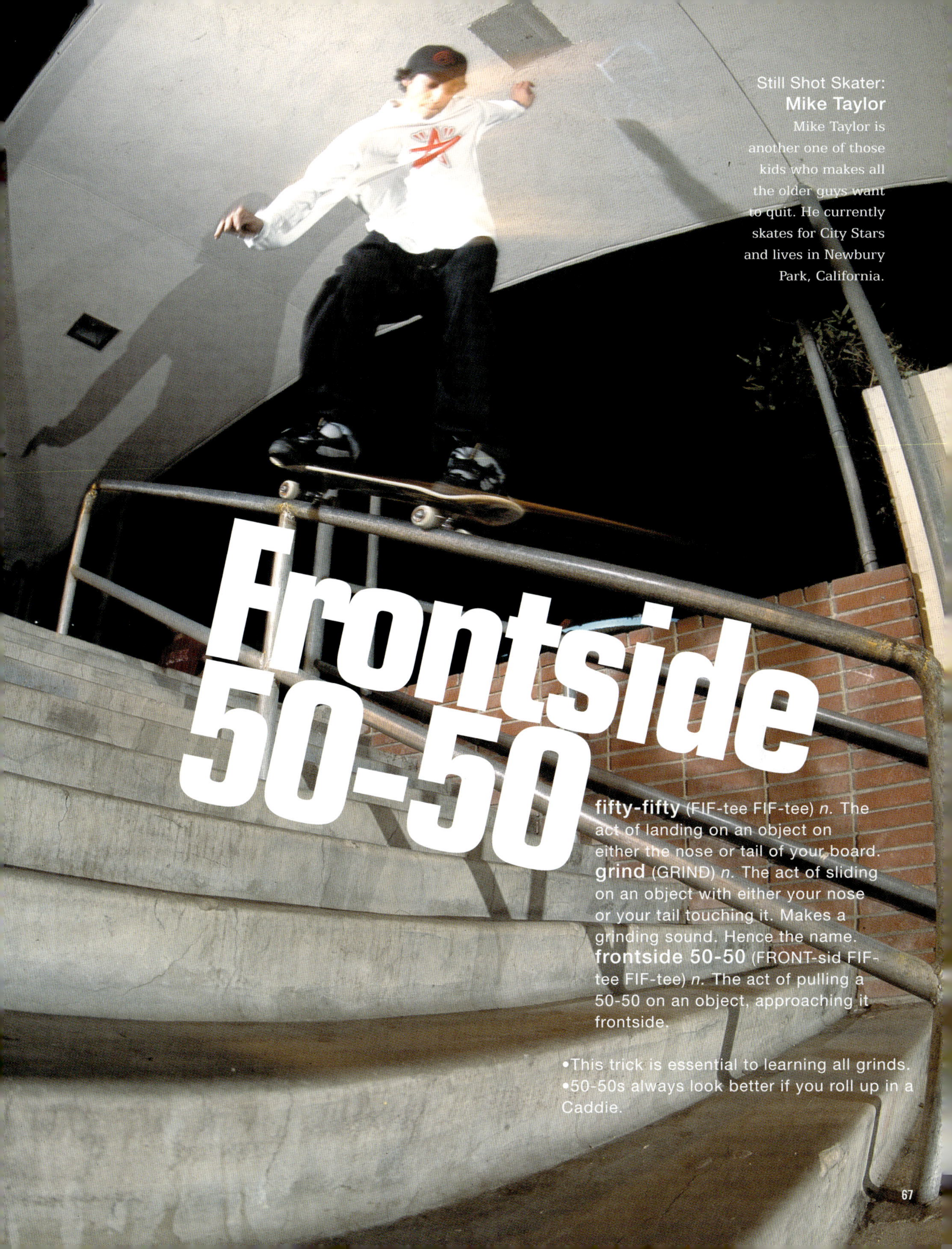

Still Shot Skater:
Mike Taylor

Mike Taylor is another one of those kids who makes all the older guys want to quit. He currently skates for City Stars and lives in Newbury Park, California.

Frontside 50-50

fifty-fifty (FIF-tee FIF-tee) *n.* The act of landing on an object on either the nose or tail of your board.
grind (GRIND) *n.* The act of sliding on an object with either your nose or your tail touching it. Makes a grinding sound. Hence the name.
frontside 50-50 (FRONT-sid FIF-tee FIF-tee) *n.* The act of pulling a 50-50 on an object, approaching it frontside.

- This trick is essential to learning all grinds.
- 50-50s always look better if you roll up in a Caddie.

Work up a moderate amount of speed and approach the obstacle from a parallel position.

Ollie. You might want to ollie up on curbs backside a few times before you learn to grind.

Make sure your back truck gets above the object. You want to try to land back truck first.

Bend your knees. This will help you balance when you lock into your grind.

Lock into your grind and keep your knees slightly bent.

When you approach the end of the grind, lift your front truck slightly to come off.

You must keep your board level and start preparing to land.

Bend your knees for impact. Land flat and keep rolling. Roll away, get in your ride, and roll out.

Sequence Skater:

Chad Muska

Chad can annihilate just about every ledge or rail he attacks with the smoothest style.

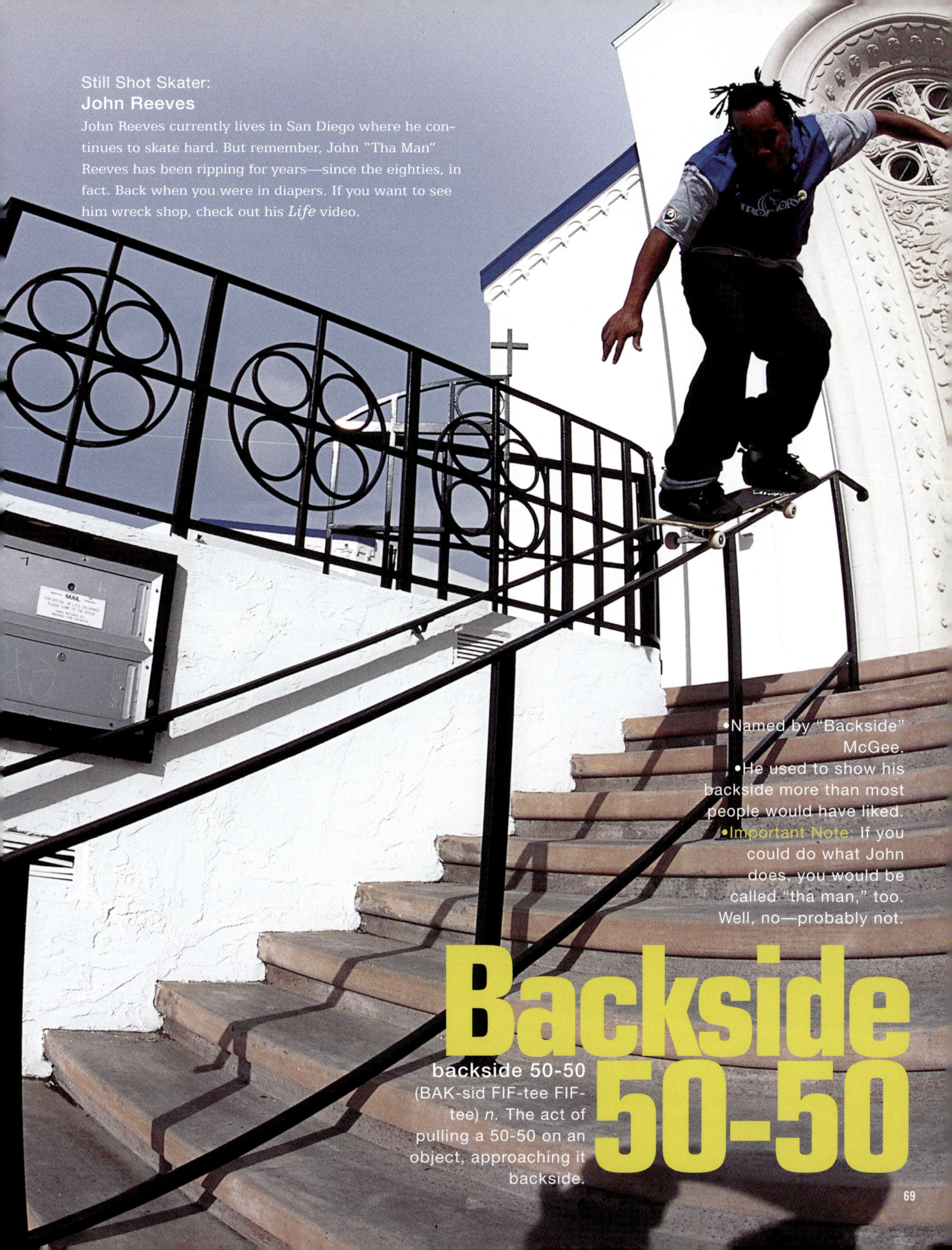

Still Shot Skater:

John Reeves

John Reeves currently lives in San Diego where he continues to skate hard. But remember, John "Tha Man" Reeves has been ripping for years—since the eighties, in fact. Back when you were in diapers. If you want to see him wreck shop, check out his *Life* video.

•Named by "Backside" McGee.

•He used to show his backside more than most people would have liked.

•Important Note: If you could do what John does, you would be called "tha man," too. Well, no—probably not.

Backside 50-50

backside 50-50 (BAK-sid FIF-tee FIF-tee) *n.* The act of pulling a 50-50 on an object, approaching it backside.

Still Shot Skater:
Trainwreck
Trainwreck, aka Alex Gall, lives in Oceanside, California, and is sponsored by Zero. Here he is, sticking up his hands like he was just caught by the cops. Is he guilty of something?

5-0 Grind

5-0 grind (FIV-OH grind) n. The act of grinding on your back truck, just like a manual.

•Sometimes when kids see the cops, they yell, "Five-oh!"
•That has nothing to do with the trick, despite Trainwreck's appearance.
•The 5-0 grind is much like standing on your toes in ballet.

Build up some speed. Crouch and prepare to ollie onto the obstacle.

With enough space between you and the obstacle, ollie—and be sure that your board clears the edge of the obstacle.

Lean back so that only your back truck lands.

Maintain balance on your back truck while you continue to grind. As you near the edge of the obstacle, prepare to dismount.

As you dismount, begin leaning forward and level out your board.

Finish leveling out your board and land on all four wheels.

Bend your knee so that you can absorb the impact. Roll away,

lookin' fly.

Sequence Skater:
Tony Tieu

Tony Tieu, aka T2

Skills: Giving fashion tips to Rico Suave.

Vital stats: Raised in San Francisco and later moved to Santa Barbara. Brought some of that northern Cali vibe with him.

Employment status: Currently the Shorty's Hardware team manager.

step 1.

Work up a good amount of speed. Ride toward the obstacle at a slight angle, not parallel—then ollie.

step 2.

Make sure you get your front truck above the obstacle.

step 3.

Land on your front truck, just like a nose manual.

step 4.

Keep your balance and grind as far as you can.

step 5.

As you reach the end, add a little more pressure to your nose.

step 6.

Pop off. Make sure your tail doesn't hit the obstacle on your way down.

Sequence Skater:
Jesse Silvey

You know Jesse from the backside 180 ollie (see page 52). Here he is, wrecking shop once more.

step 7.

Land flat.

step 8.

Roll away. Whasssuuuppp.

•Nose grinds were invented by Noser Grindeous in 1765. He invented them when he pulled a grind, got stuck, fell, and broke his nose. Poor man.
•Luckily skateboard technology has improved since then. You won't break your nose. Unless you fall.
•Don't be all snooty, kid! Stop sticking your nose in the air. Put it down there and grind.
•Learn nose manuals first. Just like Jesse did.

Nose Grind

nose grind (NOZ GRIND) *n.* The act of balancing on your back trucks and wheels while grinding.

step 1.

Make sure you wear your b-ball shorts. Bring a ball to play hoops after you pull this one.

step 2.

Approach the obstacle a little more straight on than you would with most tricks.

step 3.

Ollie onto the obstacle while eyeing the landing spot. Keep your shoulders parallel to the obstacle.

step 4.

Here's the tricky part. Land on the front truck (like a nose grind) and the nose (like a noseslide; see page 85) at the same time.

step 5.

Your board should be slightly crooked. Look at the picture—get it?!

step 6.

Grind across the obstacle. Keep your body centered over your board. Most of your weight should be on the front of the deck.

step 7.

Now the last part looks like a nollie. Just push off with your front foot. Then push down and straight.

step 8.

Now land it so fresh and so clean ... then do it switch like Dylan, so fresh and so clean ...damn, it's like dropping bombs on Baghdad.

Sequence Skater:
Dylan Gardner

Skills: Dirty D is straight underground. Dirty can break off stuff that you can't even imagine. For all who have seen him, you already know; for all who haven't, you will.

Vital stats: Representing Santa Barbara. If you haven't seen him skate, get a copy of any Church of Skatan video.

Warning: Just be ready to poo your pants. He's insane.

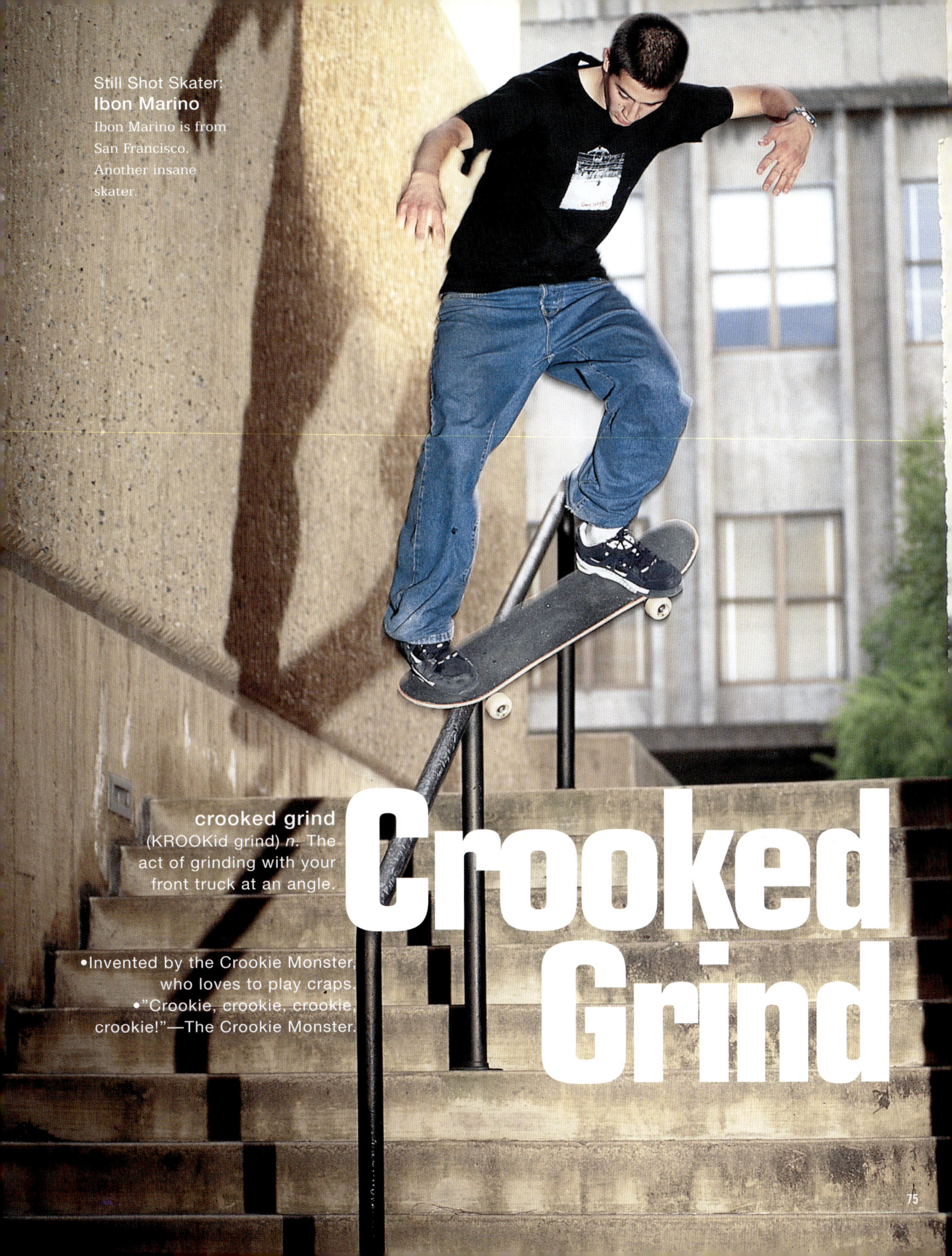

Still Shot Skater:
Ibon Marino
Ibon Marino is from San Francisco. Another insane skater.

Crooked Grind

crooked grind
(KROOKid grind) *n.* The act of grinding with your front truck at an angle.

- Invented by the Crookie Monster, who loves to play craps.
- "Crookie, crookie, crookie, crookie!"—The Crookie Monster.

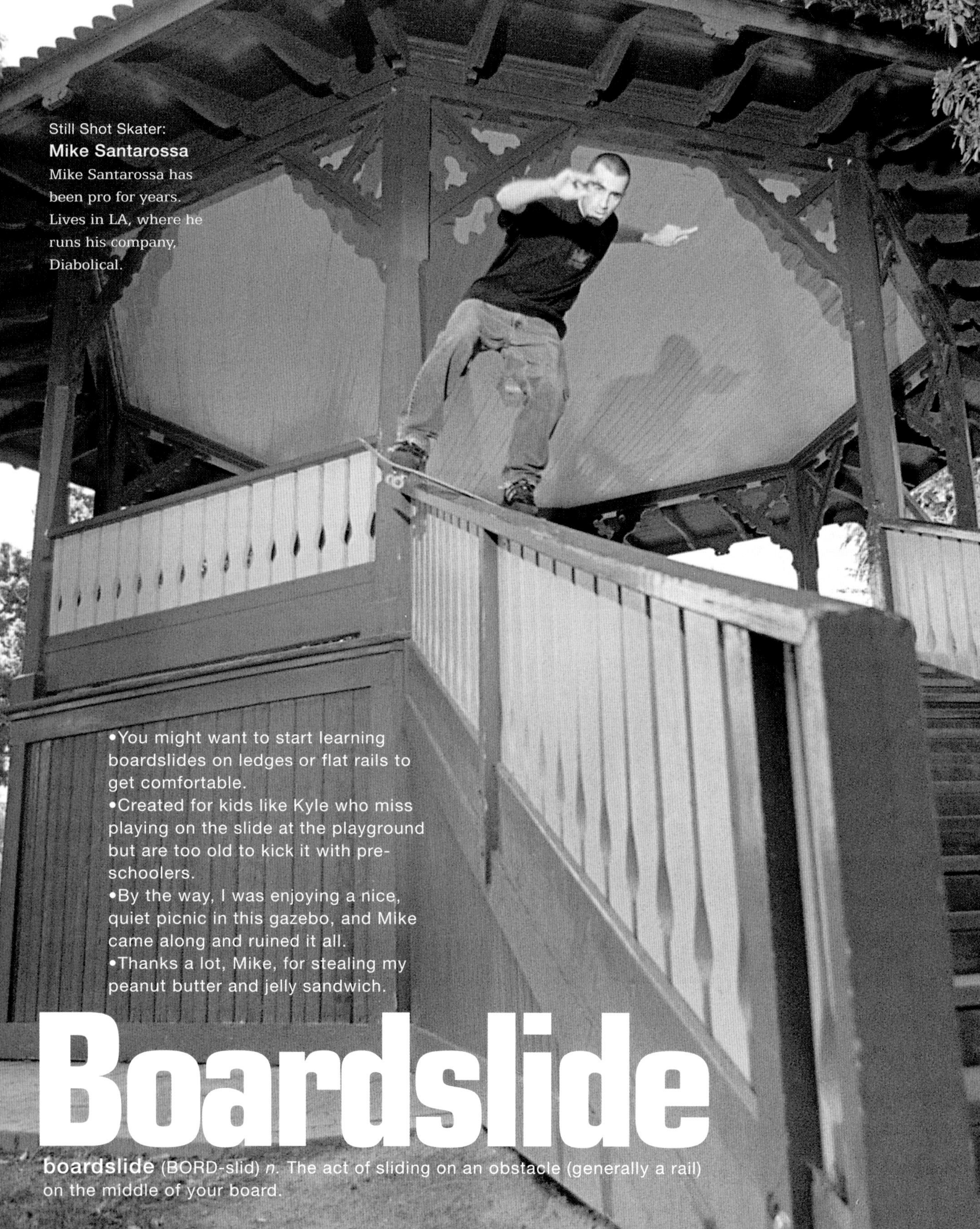

•You might want to start learning boardslides on ledges or flat rails to get comfortable.
•Created for kids like Kyle who miss playing on the slide at the playground but are too old to kick it with pre-schoolers.
•By the way, I was enjoying a nice, quiet picnic in this gazebo, and Mike came along and ruined it all.
•Thanks a lot, Mike, for stealing my peanut butter and jelly sandwich.

Boardslide

boardslide (BORD-slid) *n.* The act of sliding on an obstacle (generally a rail) on the middle of your board.

Build up a good speed. If you go too slow, you might smack your crotch on the rail.

Ollie up onto the rail and make sure that you get your front truck above it. If you bonk the truck against the rail, you might be in trouble.

Make sure you get flat on the rail because this will help you keep your balance while sliding down. You want to keep your weight a little bit forward so that you slide perpendicular to the rail.

Continue to keep your weight balanced until you are getting ready to come off.

Start turning your board and body to come off straight.

Absorb the impact by bending your knees. Stay centered and roll away. I'm only nine, fool. Where you at, huh?

Sequence Skater:
Kyle Liddle

Skills: Pissing older people off because he's so much better than them.

Vital stats: Kyle is this little nine-year-old freak from Santa Barbara.

Important note: I'm one of the people he pisses off.

Still Shot Skater:
Daniel Shimizu
Daniel Shimizu is sponsored by Foundation. Daniel can be seen skateboarding around Southern California. Check out his skills in the Foundation Video, *Art Bars.*

Frontside Boardslide

frontside boardslide
(FRONT-sid BORD-slid) *n.*
The act of sliding on an obstacle (generally a rail) on the middle of your board—but sliding backward.

• One day a skateboarder (his name is not given here for legal reasons) freaked out and hopped onto a rail backward. Later he was institutionalized. But he wasn't crazy. People simply didn't understand his twisted genius.

• Maybe someday they will.

• Matt Schook was on *Real TV* for falling over that middle knob. But in this sequence he successfully pulled the trick. We were all relieved.

• You must grow an Afro before you try a frontside boardslide.

First, find a large, ten-stair rail with big fat knobs on it. If you can't find that, then a curb or your local flatbar will do. Ollie onto the obstacle and turn your board ninety degrees at the same time.

Land on the obstacle on the middle section of your board—between the trucks.

Keep your shoulders parallel to the obstacle. The lower half of your body should be turned about ninety degrees. After you've slid as far as you want, get ready to land.

It's usually easier to come off at the end.

As you come off the rail, turn the lower half of your body straight. Make sure your board is under your feet.

Land with your feet on the bolts and ride away. If your landing is sketchy, it doesn't count. Do it again. "Whoa, whoa . . . I'm all SCHOOK up!"

Sequence Skater:
Matt Schook

Skills: Falling down and losing money.
Vital stats: Matt Schook lost all his money living in Vegas, so he came to Santa Barbara to do this frontside boardslide. Unfortunately, he didn't get paid.
Important note: He grew his hair extra long just for this photo.

Approach a ledge from a parallel position. This will give momentum to the forward motion of the noseslide. (By the way, if you don't know what parallel and perpendicular mean, go buy a dictionary. Damn, don't they teach geometry at your school?)

Ollie toward the ledge—but not all the way onto it.

Use your weight to push down on the nose. Keep your weight on your nose to slide longer. Lean back slightly; if you lean forward, you'll stop.

Get ready to pop out. Push your front foot straight to turn the board and turn your body with it. Extend your legs a little bit to take in the landing.

Sequence Skater:
Chad Muska

Nobody skates like The Muska. If you see him, you will never be the same.

Start bending your knees to take in the impact.

Land. Roll away. I am king of the world! Now do it again.

Noseslide

noseslide (NOZ-slid) *n.* The act of sliding on an obstacle (generally a ledge) on the nose of your board.

- Noseslides are fun when you have a nice view of some plants.
- Both skaters are rocking Circa brand shoes.
- Circa is Muska's shoe company.

Still Shot Skater:
Pablo Favela
Pablo Favela recently had an opening part in the newest Church of Skatan video. This kid has pop like you wouldn't believe. I mean, spec this Nza slide. Pabs is one of the O.G. kids out of Santa Barbara.

Go fast. It always helps to go fast. Also, approach the ledge at a slight angle.

Pick the spot where you want your nose to land. Keep your eye on it.

Ollie up to the ledge on the nose of your board while turning about ninety degrees.

Land on the nose of your board. This is where the "slide" part of the trick comes in. Start slidin'!

If you want to pop out and land rolling forward, keep your shoulders parallel to the ledge; if fakie, keep them perpendicular to the ledge.

When you're ready to come off and land, turn off by pushing with your front foot. Turn your board forward.

Land with your feet over the bolts—so you don't break your board—and ride away smooth. If you *do* break your board, that means you're fat. You need to go on a diet, yo.

Sequence Skater:
Jason Phillips
Jason can almost skate anything; here he breaks off a clean frontside nza.

• Also known as frontside nza's.
•Sometimes I walk backward and fall down stairs, while people like Jason and Mike pull frontside noseslides.

Frontside Noseslide

frontside noseslide (FRONT-sid NOZ-slid) *n.* The act of sliding on an obstacle (generally a ledge) on the nose of your board—but backward.

step 1.

Approach the obstacle from a parallel position. Your feet should basically be in the ollie position.

step 2.

As you pop your tail, spot where you want your tail to land.

step 3.

When you get close to your peak height, turn your board ninety degrees. Prepare to land on your tail.

step 4.

Land on your tail and prepare to slide. Keep your weight centered but most of your weight on your tail.

step 5.

To pop out rolling forward like Mike here, just turn your board back ninety degrees and land on all four wheels.

step 6.

Remember: Always try to land with your feet over the bolts. Roll away.

Sequence Skater:
Mike Lawler

Skills: Tailslides

Vital stats: Living large in Cali. Spends his days skateboarding in front of Toan's house.

Important note: Shares Toan's love for head spins and safety gear.

step 7.

That's it, baby . . . keep rollin'. Uhhuh, keep on goin'. . .

step 8.

Damn, I said roll on outta here already. Jeez!

Tailslide

tailslide (TAL-slid) *n.* The act of sliding on the tail of your board.

Lipslide

lipslide (LIPP-slid) *n.* the act of pulling a ninety-degree ollie over an obstacle (generally a rail), then landing and sliding on it on the middle of your board.

- Did you know that Revlon sells a lipstick called Lip Slide?
- This trick was named after it.
- Not really.
- Get used to doing frontside 50-50 grinds before you try a lipslide.

Approach the obstacle just as you would a frontside 50-50.

Ollie high. Make sure you get your back truck over the obstacle. If you don't, you might need some tissue when you cry.

Get your board flat over the obstacle, just like you would on a boardslide.

Lean a little forward if you're going down. This will help you keep your balance.

Sequence Skater:
Toan Nguyen
When Toan is not chillin' on his head, he breaks out the magic on the skateboard. Amazing.

Start turning your board to pop off straight. Extend your legs for impact. Bend your knees and take in the impact.

Keep rolling away till you look smooth, yo.

The Mongo's Guide to
Intermediate
Tricks

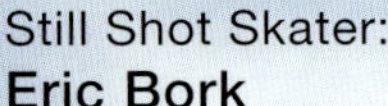

Frontside 180 Kickflip

frontside 180 kickflip (FRONT-sid WUN-A-tee KIK-flip) *n.* The act of combining the frontside 180 ollie and the kickflip.

- Tom Penny has this trick on lockdown.
- Penny has too much style.
- Bork is doing a switch frontside flip.
- Nah, I got nothing but mad love for Penny.
- You best have frontside 180 ollies and kickflips on lockdown yourself before you try this one.

Sequence Skater:
Matt Mumford

Skills: Lack of fear. Unafraid to tackle some of the burliest stuff.
Vital stats: Matt lives in Australia. In Australia, they have some of the gnarliest stuff ever to skate, and you don't even have to wear pads. There are also a lot of kangaroos down there. Did you know that Australia is the only country that is also a continent?
Board Sponsor: Zero.

step 1.

Put your feet in kickflip position. Start to ollie like you're going to pull a backside 180.

step 2.

Kick your foot off, like a kickflip, and start turning backside. Your board should simultaneously flip and turn with your body.

step 3.

You should be over your board at all times. After it's flipped, you should have already turned ninety degrees.

step 4.

Catch it with your feet.

step 5.

Turn your board another ninety degrees and prepare to land.

step 6.

Try to land nice and straight—rolling backward, with your feet on the bolts of your board.

step 7.

Roll away and give yourself a pat on the back.

Sequence Skater:
Sam Baptista
Skills: Consistency.
Vital stats: Another Santa Barbara youngster. Eighteen years old.
Board Sponsor: Shorty's.

Backside 180 Kickflip

backside 180 kickflip (BAK-sid WUN-A-tee KIK-flip) *n.* The act of combining the backside 180 ollie and the kickflip.

- Also Known as backside flizz-ips, dog.
- Backside 180 tricks just look ill.
- Arto looks like he's trying to fly back to Finland.
- Take a good look at Sam. He can do a lot of tricks. This is probably the only trick that Sam does that you have even a slim chance of pulling off. Doesn't that just suck? I mean, he's only eighteen. Important note: Whatever you do, don't try this trick right here—in this spot. The guy who lives in that house doesn't like skaters one bit. He weighs about four hundred pounds and might sit on you.

Place your right foot as you would for a kickflip, but at a slight angle.

Place your back foot as you would for a pop shove-it.

Put your left arm over your head and puff out your cheeks (that is, if you want to kick it Rico Suave style). Then pop your board like a pop shove-it.

At the same time you pop your board, kick your front foot out like a kickflip. Now let the board rotate. Keep your eye on the bolts.

When your board is done with its rotation, be ready to catch it. Find those bolts and land on them.

Land flat and bend your knees to absorb the impact, if there is any. Let the air out of your cheeks. Oh yeah, and roll away. If you want, you can fall off the curb and lie in the gutter. After your nap, try it again.

Varial Kickflip

varial kickflip (VAR-ee-all KIK-flip) *n.* The act of combining a pop shove-it and a kickflip.

Varial Heelflip

varial heelflip (VAReeall HEELflip) *n.* The act of combining a pop shove-it and a heelflip.

•You should try it on a sunny day at the beach. The ladies will be impressed. They were with Pablo.

•But don't try it if you haven't learned frontside pop shove-its and heelflips first.

Sequence Skater:
Pablo Favela

Place your front foot on your deck as you would for a heel flip. Place your back foot on the tip of your tail. Pull a frontside pop shove-it. As soon as you pop, kick out a heelflip.

Bend your knees up above the board as it rotates and flips.

Grab the board with both feet when it completes its final rotation and is done flipping.

Bend those knees to absorb the impact.

Land flat and on your bolts.

Now roll away, sucka.

step 1.

Ollie. At the same time, you want to focus on getting your back truck on the edge of the wall or ledge.

step 3.

To come out, you're going to want to pop a little ollie.

step 5.

Land with all four wheels down.

Sequence Skater:
Paul Rodriguez

Skills: Paul is doing the stuff pros are doing, and he's am.

Vital stats: Another young upstart. Paul is only sixteen, and he skates for City Stars in Los Angeles.

An interesting thing about Paul: He's the son of comedian Paul Rodriguez. Have you ever seen the movie *D.C. Cab?* It's a classic. Go rent it.

Important note: "Am" means amateur. But you probably figured that out already.

step 2.

When you're on the obstacle, shift your weight back a little bit. At the same time point your nose down. You want to keep the pressure on your back truck to stay locked in. Throw your sign in the air; wave it like you just don't care. That's what Kenny is doing. Or maybe he's just trying to keep his balance.

step 4.

Prepare to land. Bend your knees to absorb the impact.

step 6.

Roll away smooth, like the OG you are.

Still Shot Skater:
Kenny Reed
Kenny Reed lives in San Francisco and skates for New Deal. He has a smooth style. Check this stylish backside Smith grind.

Smith grind (SMITH GRIND) n. The act of grinding at an angle with your back truck below the obstacle (generally a wall or ledge).

Smith Grind

•Not invented by Will Smith.
•You don't hear a whole lot of Will Smith on my street.
•Invented by old friends Mr. Smith and Mr. Grind. They are no longer friends anymore. Mr. Grind got pissed that Mr. Smith's name came first. But Grind Smith sounds lame.
• Learn frontside 50 grinds first. This will help you with Smith grinds.

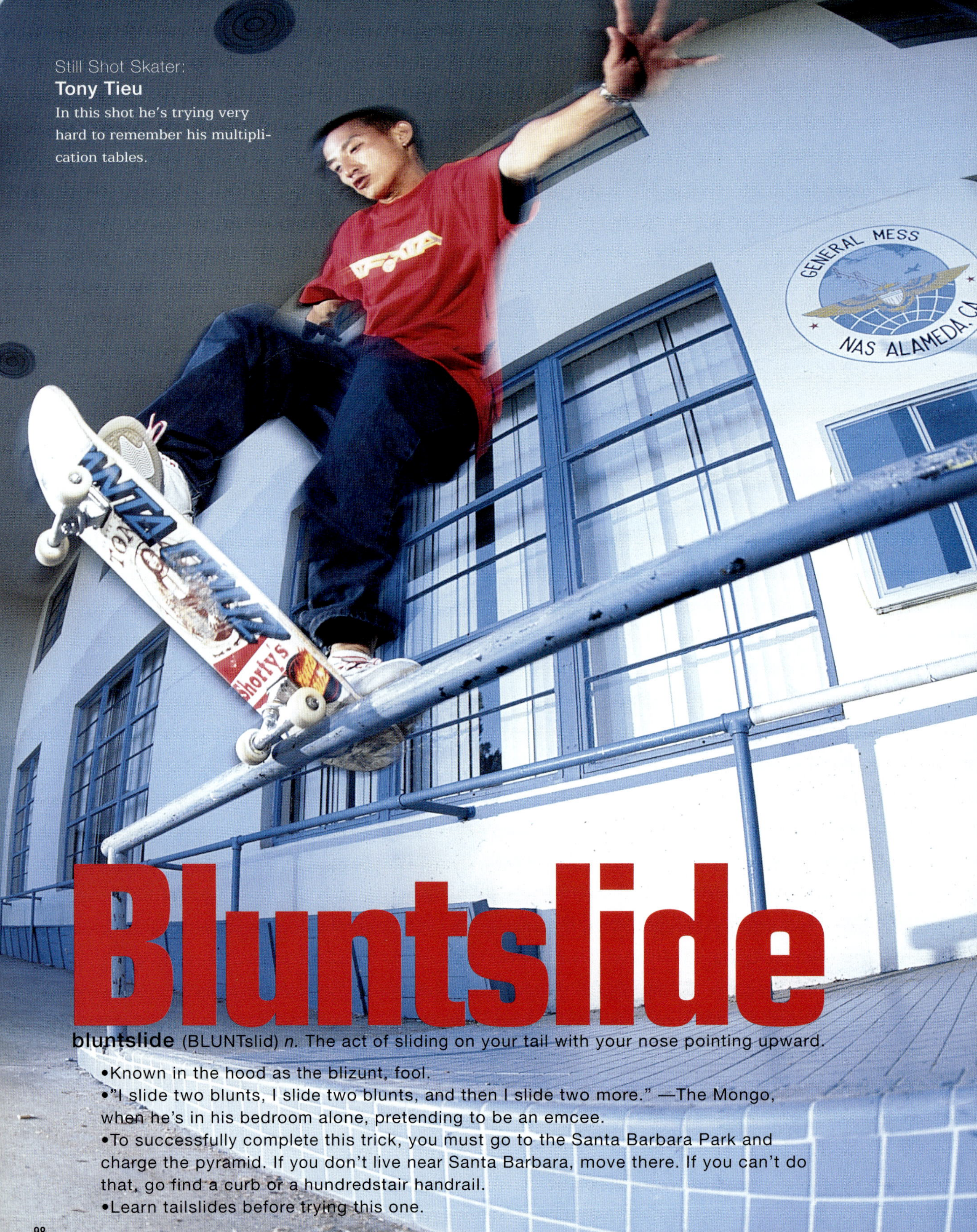

Bluntslide

bluntslide (BLUNTslid) *n.* The act of sliding on your tail with your nose pointing upward.

- Known in the hood as the blizunt, fool.
- "I slide two blunts, I slide two blunts, and then I slide two more." —The Mongo, when he's in his bedroom alone, pretending to be an emcee.
- To successfully complete this trick, you must go to the Santa Barbara Park and charge the pyramid. If you don't live near Santa Barbara, move there. If you can't do that, go find a curb or a hundredstair handrail.
- Learn tailslides before trying this one.

step 1.

Approach the obstacle backside.

step 2.

Ollie and keep your shoulders squared to the obstacle. Spot where you want to land.

step 3.

Land on the obstacle with both your back wheels and tail on the surface. Keep your weight over your board with pressure on your back foot. Slide as far as you want.

step 4.

To come out of this trick, it's a good idea to pop out like an ollie. On a rail, you want to just turn off.

step 5.

Pop out and turn your shoulders back so that they're even with the obstacle. Eye your landing area.

step 6.

Land with your feet over the bolts and on all four wheels. Roll away. Go tell your mom that you're allowed to eat anything you want for a whole week—because I said you could.

Sequence Skater:
Nick Matlin

Skills: Makes safety gear actually look cool. This is truly extraordinary.
Vital stats: Coming straight outta Florida.
Important note: Contrary to rumor, Nick was not "blunted" when he pulled this trick. Whatever "blunted" means.

step 1.

You're going to need a lot of speed for this trick, so start pushing.

step 2.

Ride almost parallel to the obstacle, then ollie up onto it as if you're going to noseslide on the opposite side.

step 3.

Make sure you lock your nose down onto the obstacle. If you don't, you'll most likely slide out. Put pressure on your front foot and use your back foot to keep the board slightly tilted.

step 4.

Now that you're on top of your board, jump off, do a really quick break dance, and then get back on.

step 5.

To come off, you're going to push down on your nose while jumping, kind of like a quick nollie.

step 6.

To come off fakie, tilt your back foot toward the fakie direction. To come off forward, tilt your back foot forward.

Sequence Skater:
Jesse Silvey

Did you know that Jesse could break-dance? No joke. He's sick.

step 7.

Straighten out your body and be ready to land flat. Bend your knees for impact.

step 8.

Now do twenty head spins and twenty worms and practice your popping. That's the key to becoming a successful break-dancer.

Nose Bluntslide

nose bluntslide (NOZ BLUNTslid) *n.* The act of sliding on your nose with your tail pointing upward.

- Also known as the nza blizunt, fool.
- Have you ever seen *Beat Street*?
- Great movie. Go watch it right now. Then you can learn this trick.

The Mongo's Guide to
Advanced
Tricks

360 Kickflip

360 kickflip (THREE-SIKS-tee KIK-flip) *n.* The act of combining a pop shove-it, a 360 rotation, and a varial kickflip.

• Also known as the "tre flip," dog.
• Get used to doing 180 varial kickflips first. It will help you get used to the rotating and landing.

step 1.

Put your foot on the tip of your tail. Now ollie and pop your back foot down and out.

step 2.

Use your front foot to guide the board, using a kickflip motion.

step 3.

Let the board rotate in between your legs.

step 4.

Now catch the board. You're going to want to keep your shoulders parallel with your feet.

Sequence Skater:
Toan Nguyen

Toan reinvents fashion in this sequence. Dig that shirt.

step 5.

Land with all four wheels. Now wave your arms frantically from side to side, just like Toan here. Bend your knees and take in the impact. Roll away. Keep rolling away if you want to. Sometimes I just keep rolling and rolling. These Black Panthers are just too damn good.

Hard Flip

step 1.

step 2.

step 3.

Place your feet on the board as you would for a frontside 180 kickflip.

Pop the board and let it flip in between your legs. (Watch out for your sensitive areas, know what I'm sayin'?)

Bend your knees up high and keep them above the board. Allow the board to complete its rotation.

•This trick was named the hard flip 'cause when people like Ben do it, they look hard.
•Also dubbed the "hard flip" because it's extremely difficult. In fact, it's so hard that you'll never, ever do it—until you have finished reading every page of this book.
•It's essential that you master frontside 180 kickflips first. That trick will teach you how to flip the board.

step 4.

Now it's time to catch the board. When you see the grip tape, catch it with your feet. Keep your knees bent to absorb the impact of landing.

step 5.

Land flat with your feet on the bolts and all four wheels touching the ground.

step 6.

Now kiss your knees and roll away. Okay, that wasn't so hard, was it?

Sequence Skater:
Ben Kendall
Ben has to wear a helmet sometimes-he already has been dropped a few too many times on his head; it's a little soft.

Nollie Heelflip

Place your feet in the nollie heelflip position.

Pop your nollie. At the same time kick out your back foot in a heelflip.

Stay centered over the board as it rotates. Keep an eye on the rotation and be ready to catch the board.

nollie heelflip (NOL-lee HEEL-flip) *n.* The act of combining a nollie and a heelflip.

- A match made in heaven.
- This trick is fun.
- When you get your nollie heels down, go combine a nollie heelflip with a crooked grind and have fun.
- But first you must master both the nollie and the heelflip. Otherwise you're frontin'.

As the board makes its final rotation, grab it with your feet.

Keep your knees bent so that when you land, you can be ready to absorb the impact.

Land flat with all four wheels touching the ground and roll away. All right. Now that you've learned that trick, practice it with crooked grinds down twenty-five-stair handrails. But keep the cellie handy for that 911 call.

Sequence Skater:
Pat Chanita
Skills: The illest tricks.
Vital stats: So-Cal all the way. Pat has won a bunch of contests in the last few years and has been holding down on the streets since the days when he was sponsored by Plan B.
Board Sponsor: Powell.

Alley-oop Lien Air

alley-oop lien air (AL-lee-OOP LEEN AIR) *n.* The act of combining a frontside 360 ollie with a lien grab.

step 1.

step 2.

step 3.

Get a good amount of speed and ollie like you would on a frontside 180—except that you're going to have to keep rotating.

Suck up that ollie and grab your board in between your legs with your front hand.

Continue rotating while grabbing your board at the same time. Hold that grab. It doesn't count as a grab if you only touch it with your fingertips.

• Tricks like this are too damn fun. Learn this trick.

• Hold up. First, learn frontside 360 ollies. Second, learn lien grabs (see the Grab Glossary, fool). Okay, now you're ready.

Sequence Skater:
Geoff Rowley
Skills: Getting very high into the air.
Vital stats: Geoff is from Liverpool, England (the home of the Beatles, in case you were wondering). He came to the States with the Flip Team and just exploded onto the American skateboard scene. Geoff now lives in Huntington Beach.

step 4.

Be ready to complete that final 180. At this point you can release your grab.

step 5.

Keep your knees slightly bent to take in the impact. Turn your board to land straight and flat.

step 6.

Land flat and roll away. *Now* who's the man?

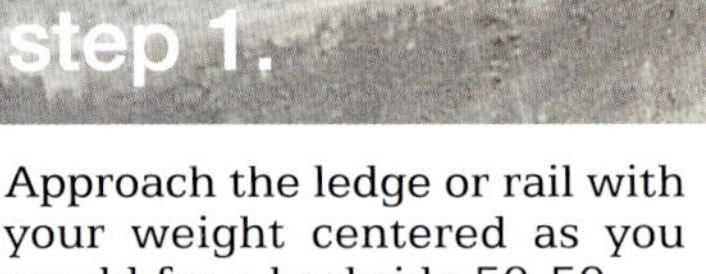

Approach the ledge or rail with your weight centered as you would for a backside 50-50.

Ollie up and over the ledge or rail. Then turn ninety degrees backside to land in the backside position.

Do not drastically shift your weight. You will basically be standing up straight at this point, so you should continue to stay in this position. Slide.

Sequence Skater:
Arto Saari

Backside Lipslide

backside lipslide
(BAK-sid LIP-slid) *n.* The act of combining an ollie, a frontside boardslide, and a backside 50-50. Sort of.

When you're done with your slide, apply the correct pressure to your board to come off straight.

Turn your board and straighten it out.

Land flat and roll away. Nice job.

•This trick is so damn hard that it's nearly impossible to define.
•Arto breaks this trick off.
•Backside lipslides have been taken to the next level recently. Arto has been one of those guys to do just that.
•A backside lipslide is one of the most awkward tricks to master. Learn frontside boardslides and backside 50-50s to help.

FOOT PLACEMENT

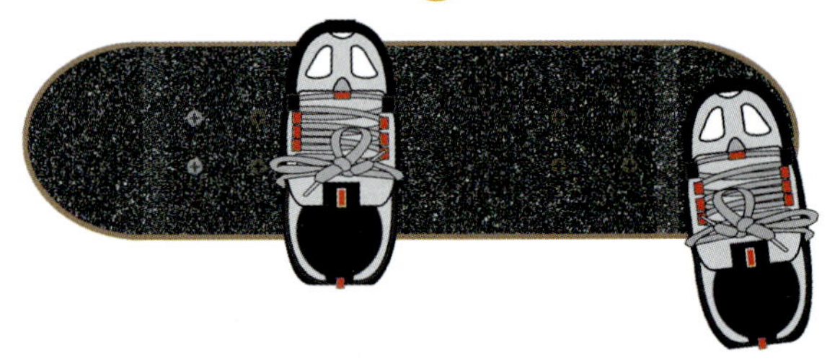
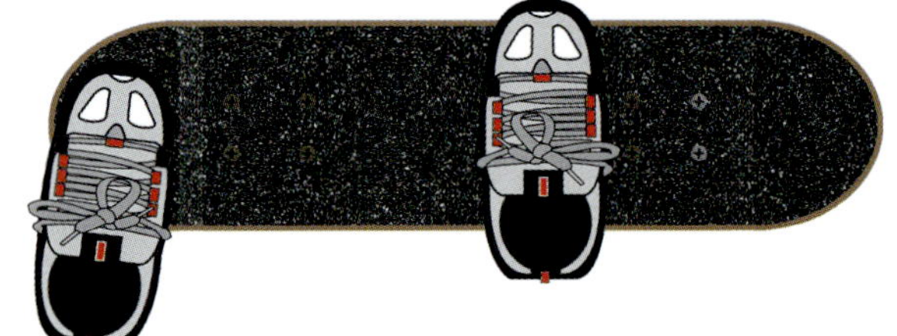

Ollie

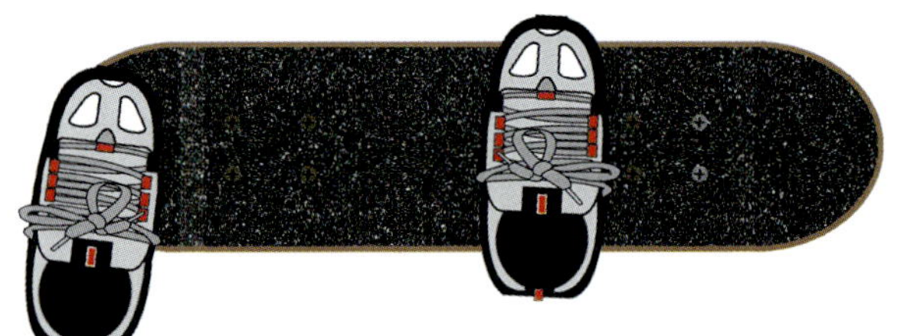

Frontside 180 Ollie

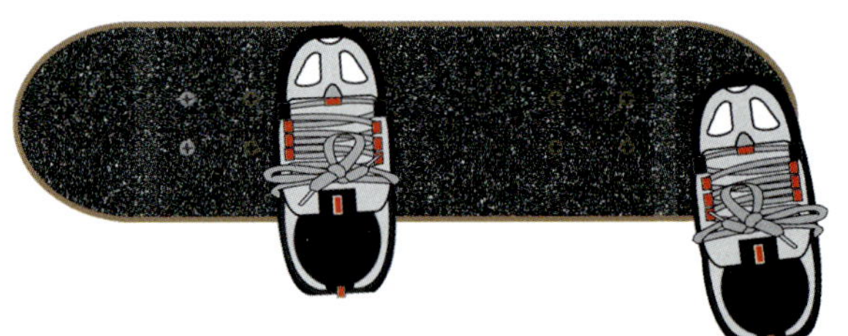
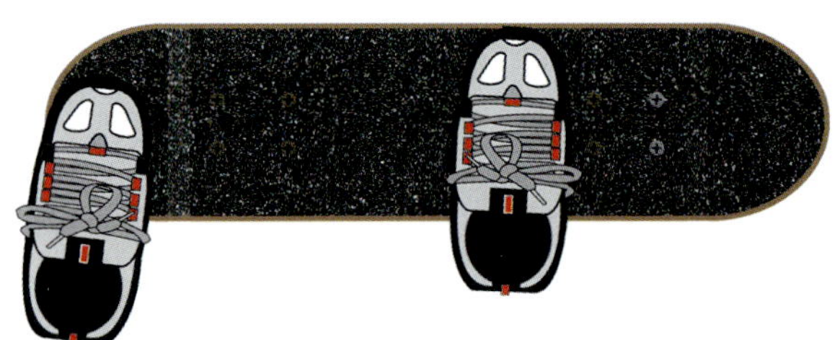

Backside 180 Ollie

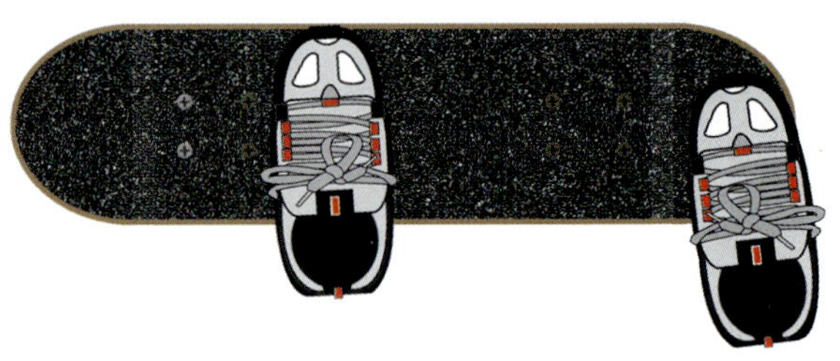
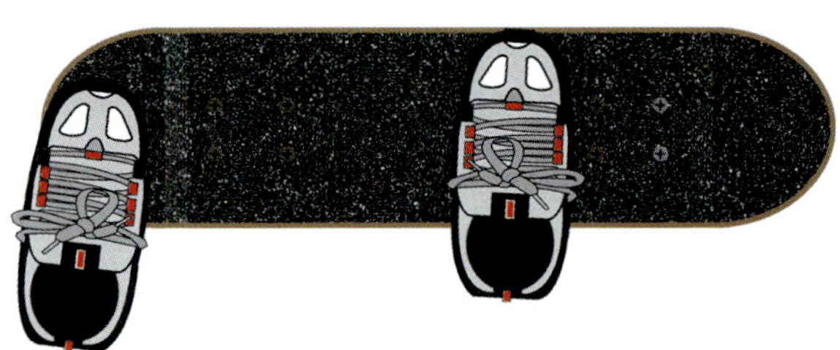

Half Cab

GLOSSARY

Pop Shove-it

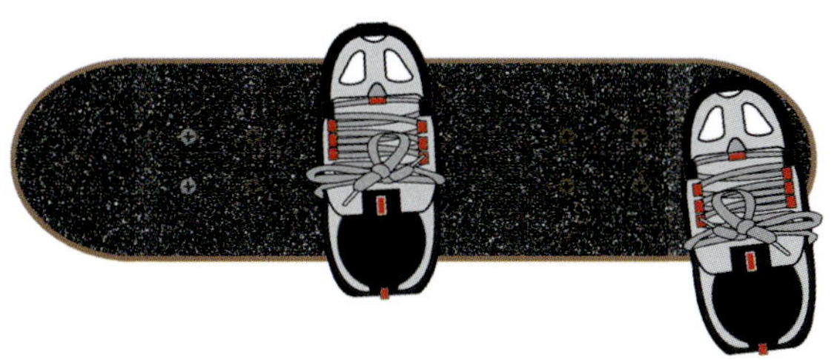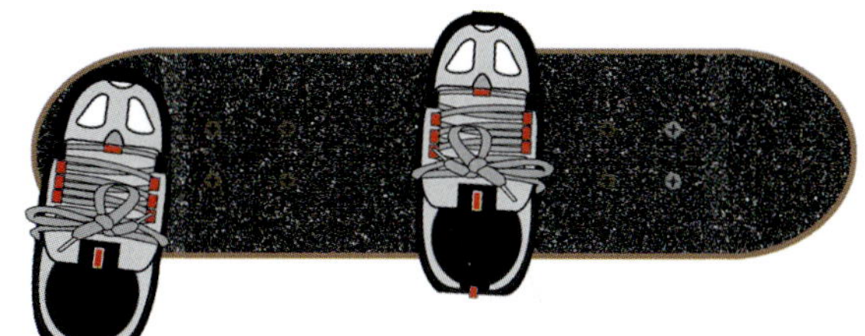

Manual

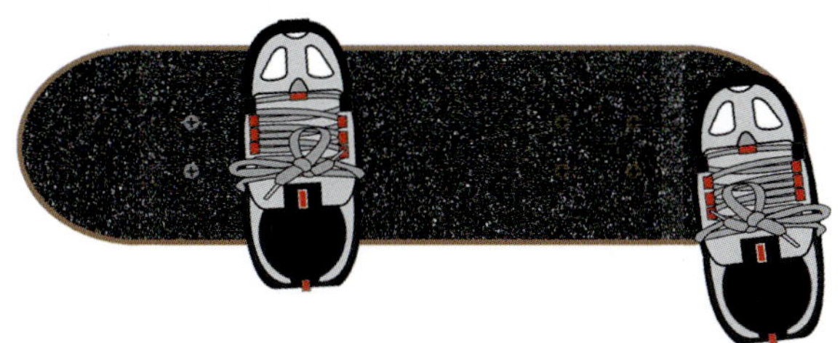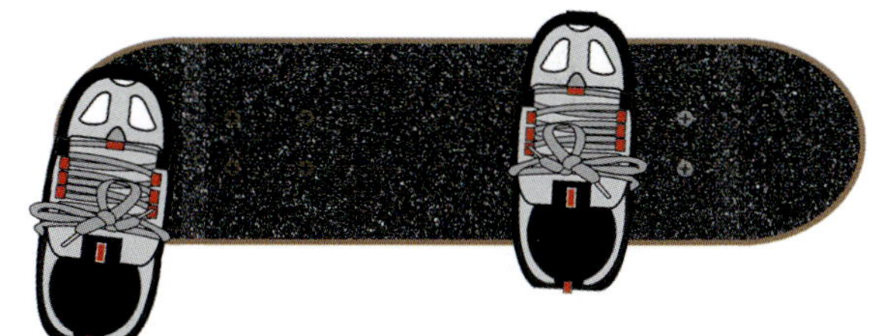

Nose Manual

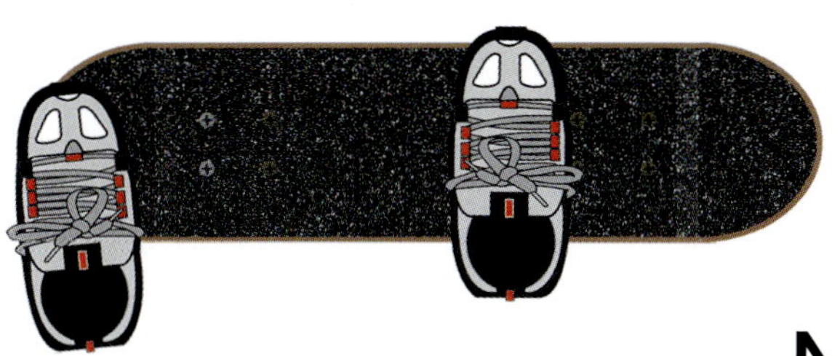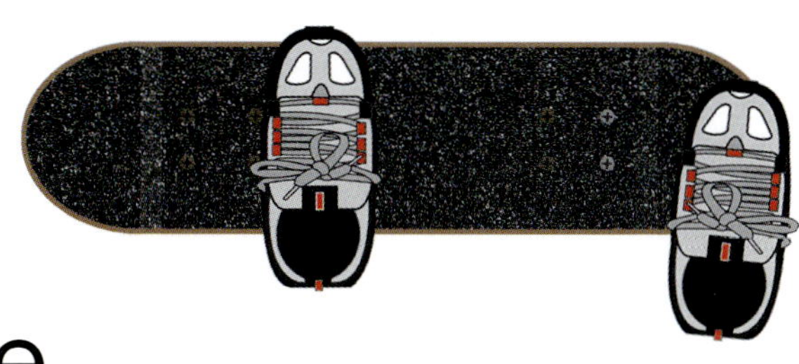

Nollie

Kickflip

Heelflip/Varial Heelflip

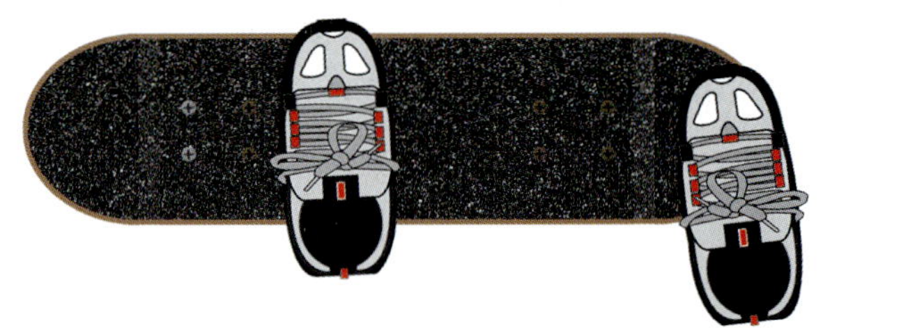
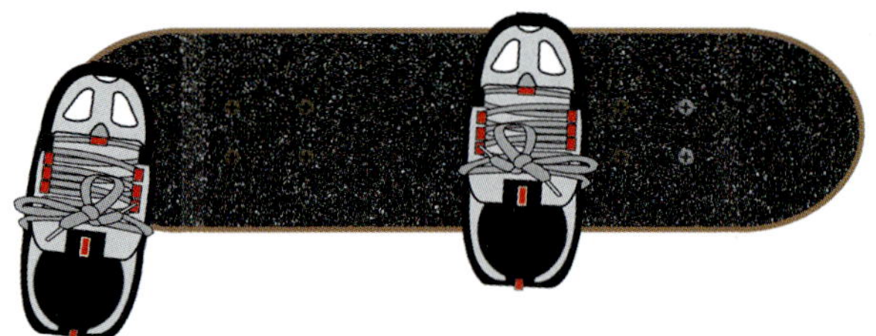

Frontside 50-50

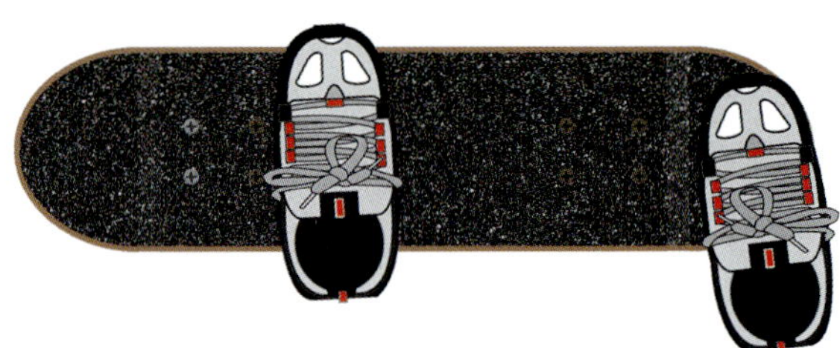
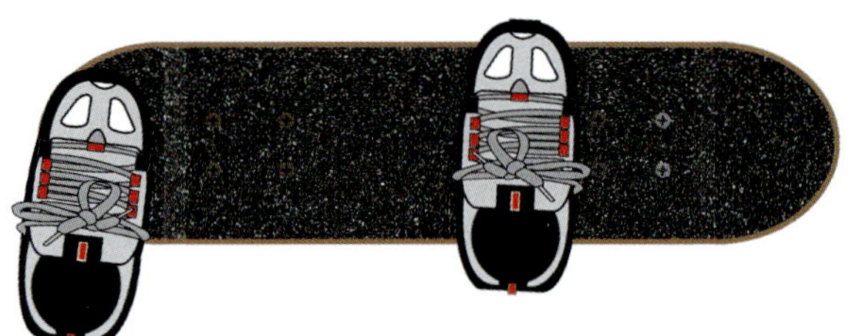

Backside 50-50

5-0 Grind

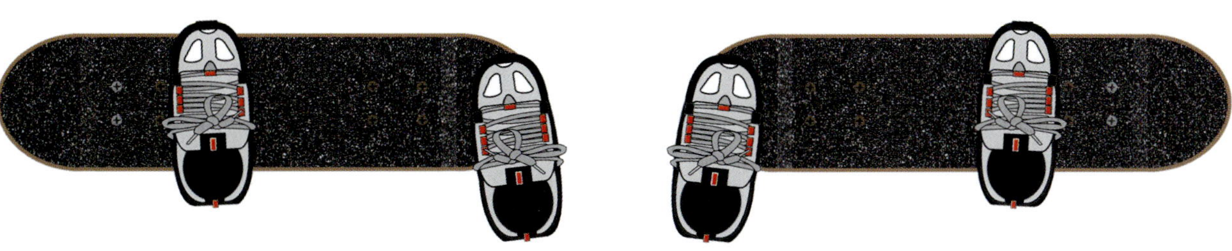

Nose Grind

Crooked Grind

Boardslide

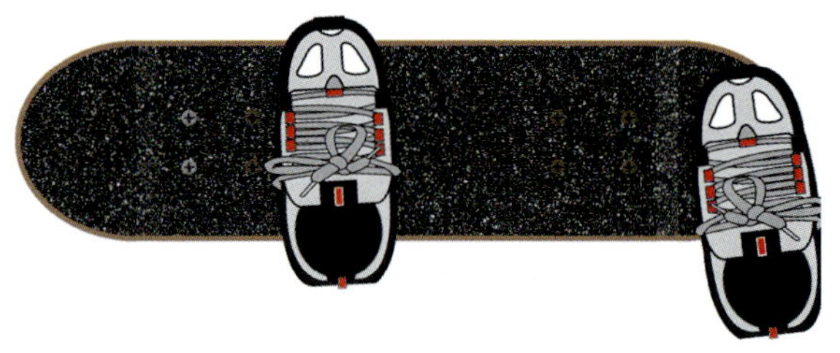 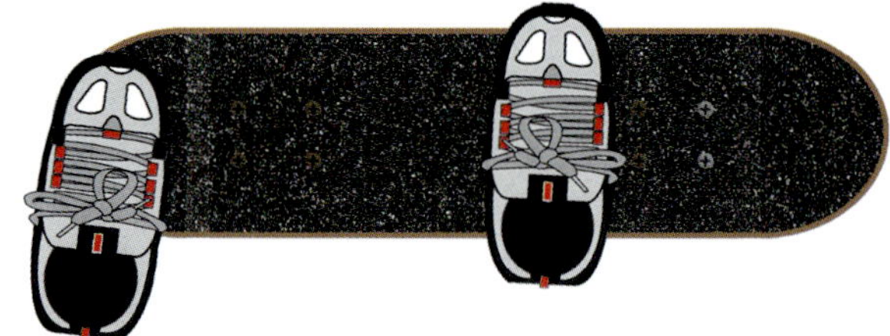

Frontside Boardslide

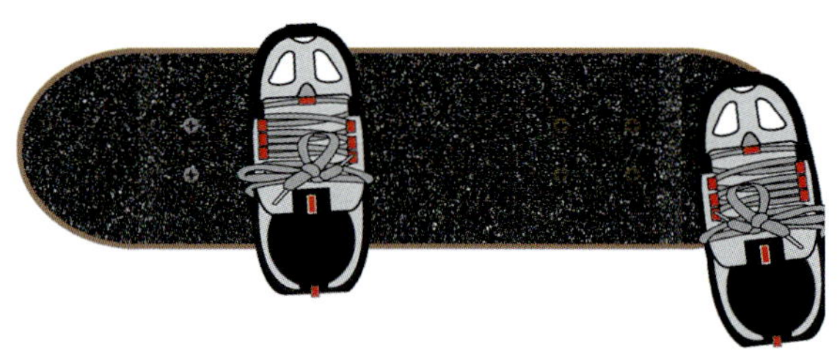 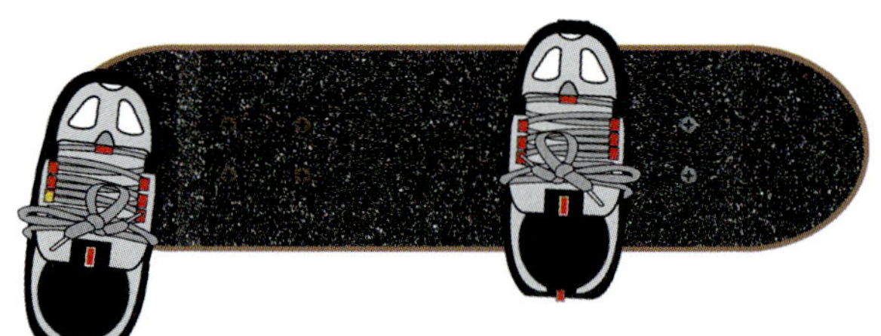

Noseslide

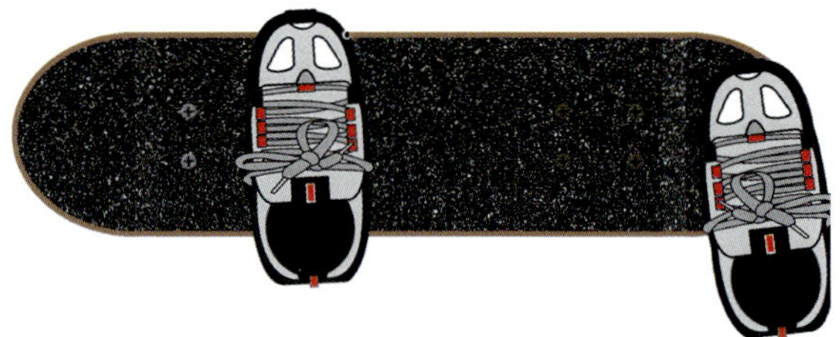 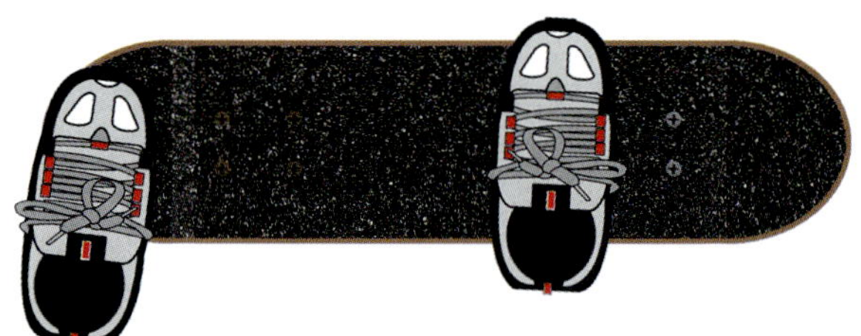

Frontside Noseslide

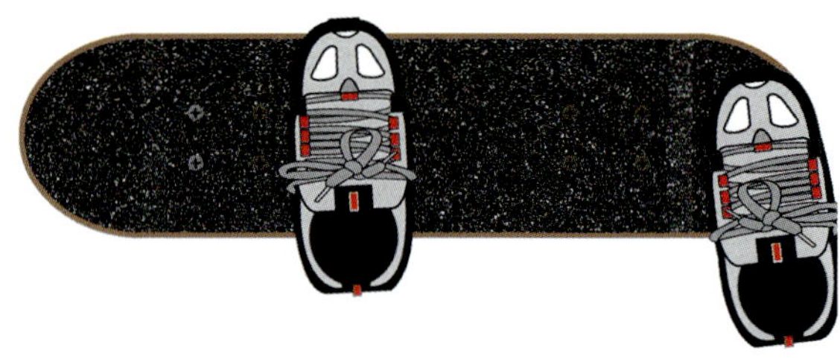 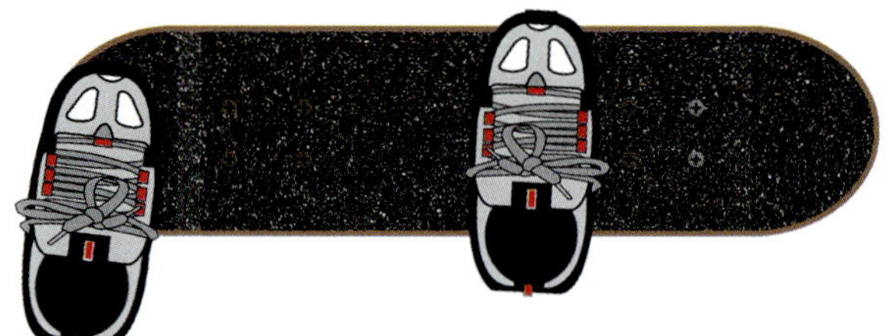

Tailslide

Lipslide

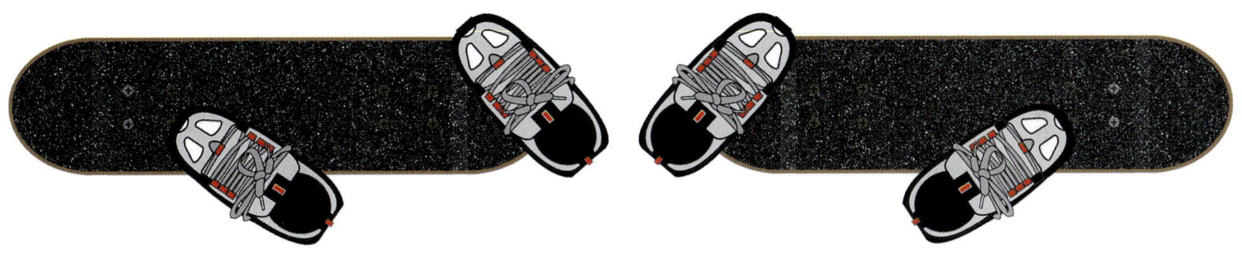

Frontside 180 Kickflip

Backside 180 Kickflip

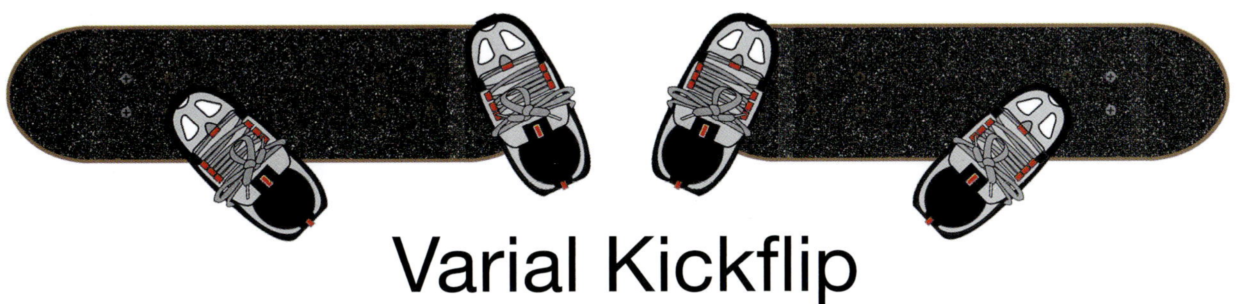

Varial Kickflip

Smith Grind

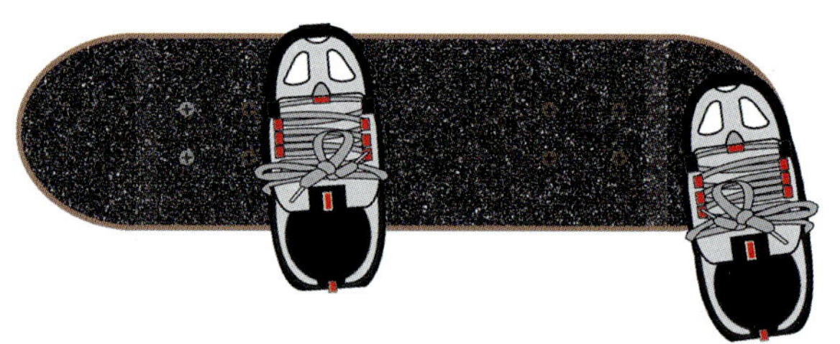
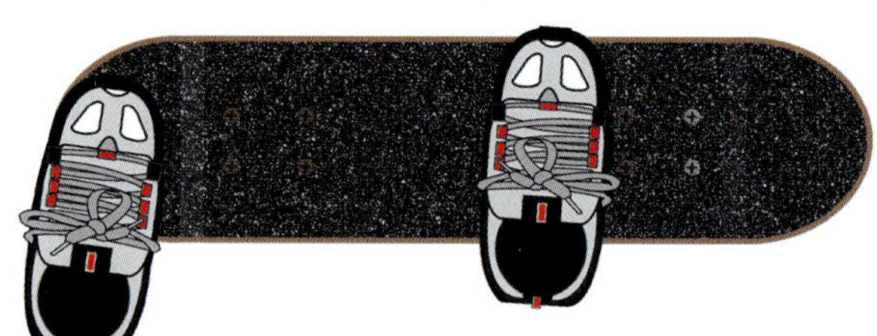

Bluntslide

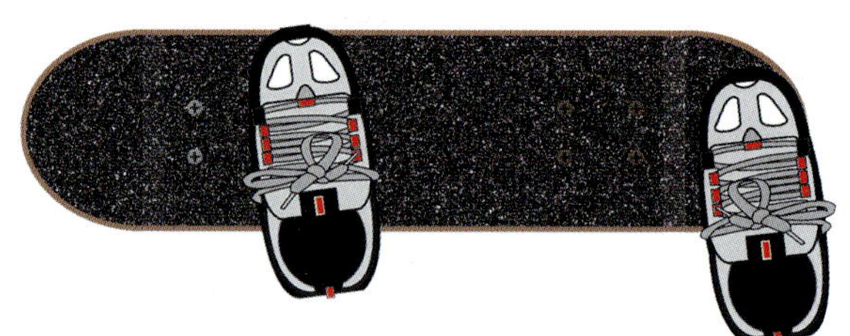
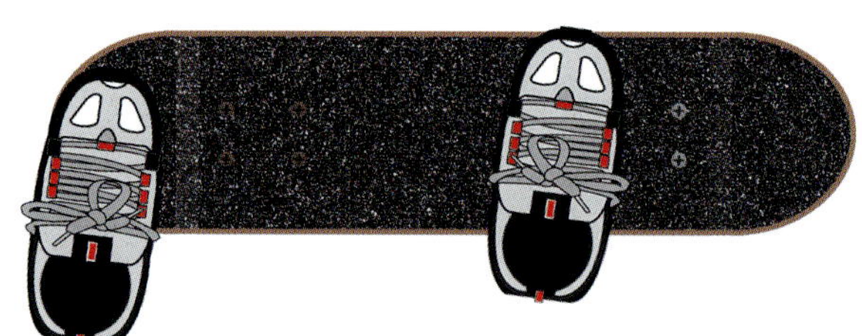

Nose Bluntslide

360 Kickflip

Hard Flip

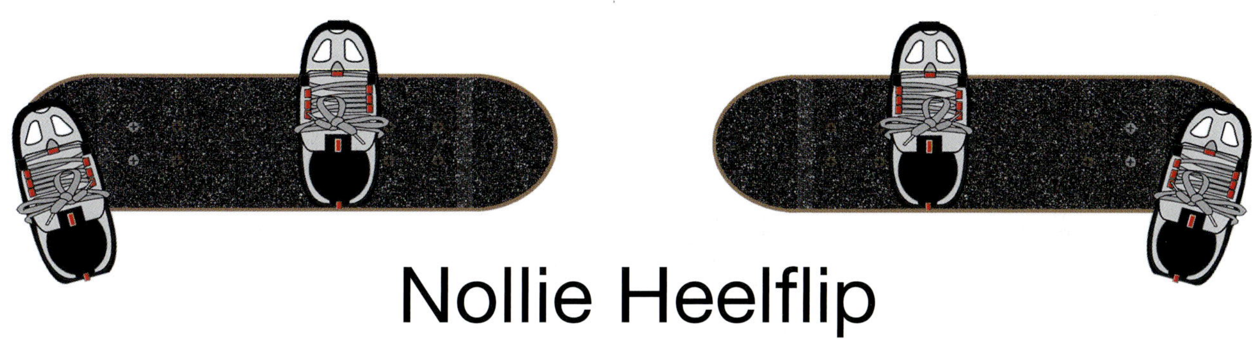

Nollie Heelflip

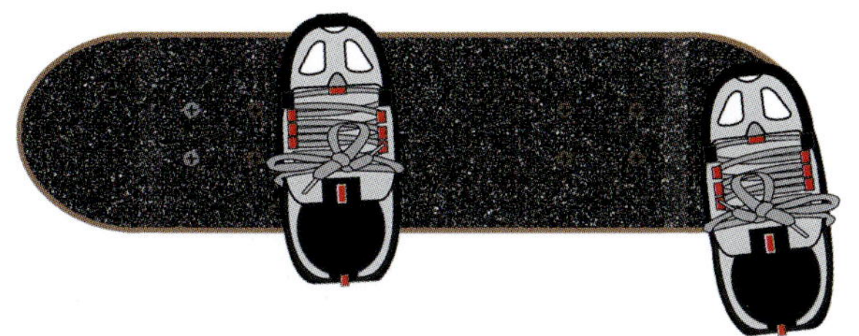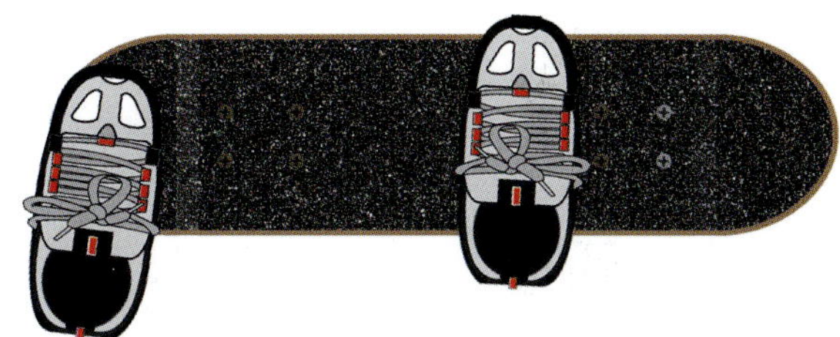

Alley-oop Lien Air

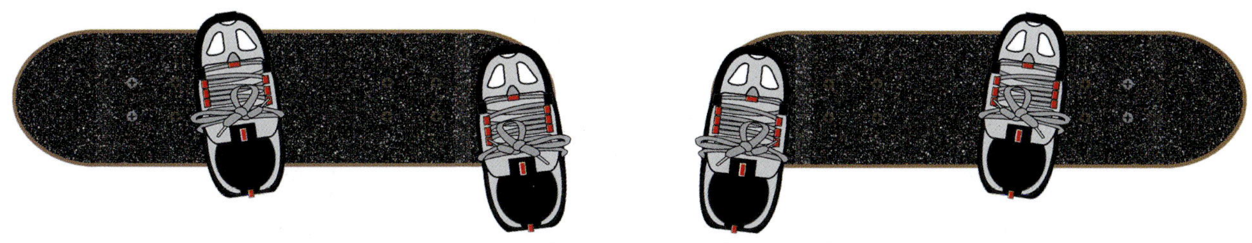

Backside Lipslide

GRAB GLOSSARY

With Judas

Tail grab: When your back hand grabs your tail.

Stale fish: When you use your back hand to grab behind your back leg in the middle of your board.

Nose grab: When you use your front hand to grab your nose.

Backside grab (also known as the lien grab): When you use your front hand to grab the middle of your board (not as pictured above).

Ya dogg grab: When you grab in between your legs with your front hand and grab the backside of your board with your back hand.

Frontside grab: When you use your back hand to grab the middle of your board.

Ham on Rye grab: When you use your back hand and grab in between your legs.

Constipated grab: When you grab your nose and tail at the same time and make a face like you're having problems with the plumbing.

Monkey grab: When you use both hands to grab the middle of your board.

GOLETA UNION
SCHOOL DISTRICT
Powr-Flite

LIFE = SKATEBOARDING

Well, you've finished the book. Congratulations are due again. You now have a bright future ahead of you. Like your guide, The Mongo, you have achieved wisdom and enlightenment. You know how to use a helmet for head spins and how to beat your friends down with a frying pan . . . and soon, with enough practice, you'll be able to pull all the tricks in this book. If you work hard enough at anything, you can do anything—even become a janitor. Don't laugh! Because as a janitor who also skates, you can secretly open the halls you clean to other skateboarders. You see? You are part of a movement now—working with others to turn the world into a giant skate park, one small step at a time. And always remember that skateboarding is not about going pro, or getting sponsored, or being the best. It's about being an individual. Skateboarding is an art and a culture. Express it and express yourself. And never stop, because life is not about having a nine-to-five job and wallowing in misery at a desk. Life is about fun. So live it. SKATE.

Credits

Created and written by Benny Bermudez
Photographer: Erik Hatch
Contributing photographers: David Broach, Brian Uyeda, Mike Burnett, Shelby Woods, John Bradford, Psycho Mike
Contributing writers: Manabu Kamukara, Erik Hatch
Contributing Artist: Ajana Green
Contributing Hair: Carlos Juarez
Almighty Corrector: Tony Tieu
Japanese Translator: Manabu Kamukara
Special thanks to the skateboarders:

Jake Stewart, Stacy Lowery, Jason Phillips, Gerardo Mendoza, Ben Kendall, Levi Marvin, Joey Pulsifer, Brandon Turner, Mark Appleyard, Damian Bravo, Peter Smolik, Erik Bork, Carlos Juarez, Chad Muska, Trainwreck, Tony Tieu, Jesse Silvey, Karl Watson, Dylan Gardner, Ibon Marino, Mike Taylor, Mike Santarossa, Kyle Liddle, Matt Schook, Daniel Shimizu, Sean Sheffey, Pablo Favela, Mike Rafter, Mike Lawler, Pete McGeary, Toan Nguyen, Matt Mumford, Sam Baptista, Arto Saari, Kenny Reed, Nick Matlin, Henry Sanchez, Pat Chanita, Geoff Rowley, John Reeves, Paul Rodriguez, Brian Hoard.

Extra-special thanks: Erik Hatch, David "Kak" Broach, Brian Uyeda, Mike Burnett, Shelby Woods, John Bradford, Psycho Mike, Manabu, Tony Tieu, Gerardo, Paul Blahnik, Tony Buyalos, April Hamrick, Chad Muska, Shorty's, Ghetto Child, Vern and Ryan at Circa, Noe Flores, Carlos Juarez, Toan Nguyen, Dewi Lim, Laurie Cherry, Jerry Bermudez, Ajana Green, Bodhi Oser, Russ and Dave at CCS, all the Ortega kids, Presidio Players, 17th Street Productions, Chris Liddle, Church of Skatan, everyone who buys this book . . .

Thanks to the SB Crew: Erik, Noe, Carlos, T2, Manabu, Joe, Broach, Nunes, George, Jake, Jim, Josh, and Karl.

Thanks to the Carpas Homies: Fat Larry, Adam, Shaina, and Mario.

I am sorry if I left anyone out!!! Thank you!!! I appreciate everything!!!

Opportunities are presented every day. You just have to keep your eyes open to see them. Create your life, and don't let life create you. Find that dream and fulfill it.

Yeah, now you know how to pull sick tricks. So you need a board to match your skills. Quit lagging, yo! Enter to win a killer skateboard at

strengthmag.com
(http://www.strengthmag.com).

Skate! Sweepstakes
Official Rules

1. Entry: NO PURCHASE NECESSARY. A PURCHASE DOES NOT IMPROVE YOUR CHANCES OF WINNING. VOID WHERE PROHIBITED BY LAW. Enter by completing the official registration form (pursuant to The Privacy Statement and the Children's Online Privacy Protection Act (COPPA) on the Sweepstakes page located at http://strengthmag.com, or if you want to enter by mail, see below. If you are not an existing Strength member, you will be asked to register for a free ID through on-screen directions which shall request your first and last name, mailing address, and e-mail address. Sweepstakes begins October 1, 2001, at 12:01 AM Eastern time and ends December 31, 2001, at 11:59 PM Eastern time. Automated or robotic entries submitted by individuals or organizations will be disqualified.
To enter by mail, send a 3x5 card on which you have hand-printed your first and last name, address, telephone number and e-mail address (if available) to: "Skate! Sweepstakes" Mail-ins, Strength Magazine, 151 West 26th Street, 11th Floor, New York, New York 10001. All mail-in entries must be received no later than January 9, 2002. Only one entry accepted per person, regardless of entry method.

2. Privacy: By entering into the Sweepstakes, you agree to Strength's use of your personal information as described in CCS's Privacy Statement at http://ccs.com.

3. Eligibility: Only U.S. residents thirteen years or older as of December 31, 2001 are eligible to enter this Sweepstakes. Void where prohibited by law. Employees of Alloy Online, Inc., Phase Three, Inc. dba CCS ("CCS") Strength Magazine ("Strength") their respective parents, affiliates, subsidiaries, suppliers, printers, distributors, advertising and promotional agencies, prize suppliers and the immediate family or household members of each are not eligible to participate or win.

4. Winner Selection: The winner will be determined from a random drawing from among all eligible entries January 10, 2002, to be conducted by Strength designated judges, whose decisions are final. Winners will be notified by e-mail or by mail, depending on entry method, on or about January 11, 2002. Odds of winning depend on the number of eligible entries received. The potential prizewinner and, if the potential prizewinner is under the age of 18, the potential prizewinner's parent or guardian, will be required to sign an affidavit of eligibility and release of liability within fourteen (14) days of notification. In the event of non-compliance within this time period, an alternate winner will be selected. No substitution or transfer of the prize is permitted except by CCS/Strength. CCS/Strength is not responsible, and may disqualify an entrant if the entrant's e-mail does not work or is changed without prior notice by email to sschneibolk@alloy.com.

5. Prize:
One (1) Custom Skateboard and Safety Helmet – Winner will receive a custom skateboard assembled and provided by CCS. Styles, boards and components shall be selected by CCS. Strength reserves the right to substitute a prize for another of comparable monetary value. CCS AND STRENGTH ALWAYS RECOMMEND THE USE OF PROTECTIVE GEAR. APPROXIMATE RETAIL VALUE: $150.00.

6. General Conditions: This Sweepstakes is governed by the laws of the United States. All federal, state and local laws and regulations apply. The Sweepstakes is not to be used in connection with any form of gambling. Prize will only be awarded and/or delivered to addresses within the United States. All taxes, fees, and surcharges are the sole responsibility of the prize winner.

Except where prohibited by law, the winner (and parent/legal guardian if winner is a minor) grants (and agrees to confirm that grant in writing) permission for Strength, its advertising and promotional agencies, and those acting under its authority to use such winner's name, photograph, voice and/or likeness, for advertising and/or publicity purposes in all media now known or hereafter discovered, worldwide and on the world wide web, without notice, review, approval, or additional compensation. Entrants further agree that Strength, CCS, their respective parents, subsidiaries and affiliated companies, advertising and promotion agencies, suppliers, printers, distributors, and the respective officers, directors, employees, representatives and agents of each will have no liability whatsoever for, and shall be held harmless by entrants (and parent/legal guardian if entrant is a minor) against, any and all liability for any injuries, loss or damage of any kind to persons, including death, or property damage resulting in whole or in part, directly or indirectly, from acceptance, possession, misuse or use of any prize, participation in this promotion, or while traveling to, preparing for or participating in any prize-related activity. Strength and CCS expressly disclaim any responsibility or liability for injury or loss to any person or property relating to the delivery and/or subsequent use of any prize item awarded. Strength and CCS make no representation or warranty concerning the appearance, safety or performance of any prize awarded. Restrictions, conditions, and limitations apply. Strength will not replace any lost or stolen prize items.

7. Conduct: By entering this Sweepstakes, entrants agree to be bound by these official rules. The official rules will be posted at the sweepstakes site throughout the sweepstakes. Entrants further agree to be bound by the decisions of the judges, which are final and binding in all respects. Strength reserves the right at its sole discretion to disqualify any individual it finds to be tampering with the entry process or the operation of the sweepstakes or website; to be acting in violation of the official rules; or to be acting in an unsportsmanlike or disruptive manner, or with intent to annoy, abuse, threaten or harass any other person.

8. Limitations of Liability: CCS and Strength are not responsible for lost or misdirected mail, technical hardware or software failures of any kind, lost or unavailable network connections, misdirected e-mail, or failed, incomplete, garbled or delayed computer transmission which may limit a user's ability to participate in the sweepstakes.

CCS and Strength reserve the right to cancel or modify the on-line portion of the sweepstakes or disqualify an entrant if fraud, misconduct or technical failures destroy the integrity of the sweepstakes as determined by Strength, in its sole discretion.

Any attempt by an entrant or any other individual to deliberately damage any website or undermine the legitimate operation of the sweepstakes is a violation of criminal and civil laws and should such an attempt be made, Strength and CCS reserve the right to seek damages from any such person to the fullest extent permitted by law. In such event or in the event a potential winner entered by the internet and a dispute arises regarding the specific individual entitled to receive a prize, entries made by the internet will be declared made by the authorized account holder and any damage made to the website will also be the responsibility of the authorized account holder of the e-mail address submitted at the time of entry. "Authorized account holder" is defined as the person who is assigned to an e-mail address by an internet access provider, online service provider or other organization that is responsible for assigning e-mail addresses for the domain associated with the submitted e-mail address.

Strength and CCS are not responsible for any liability or damage to any computer system resulting from participation in, or accessing or downloading information in connection in connection with this sweepstakes.

9. Winner's List: The name of the winner will be posted at strengthmag.com by January 11, 2002 and is available by mail after January 12, 2002, by sending a self-addressed, stamped, #10 envelope to: Strength Magazine, 151 West 26th Street, 11th floor, NY, NY 10001, attn: Skate! Sweepstakes Winner. Residents of Vermont and Washington may omit postage.

10. Official Rules: For a mailed copy of the official game rules, send a self-addressed, stamped envelope before December 31, 2001 to: Strength Magazine, 151 West 26th Street, 11th floor, NY, NY 10001, attn: Skate! Sweepstakes Rules. Residents of Vermont and Washington may omit return postage.